the miracles of
mary

Bridget Curran

the miracles of mary

everyday encounters
of beauty and grace

inspired
LIVING

ALLEN&UNWIN

First published in 2008
Copyright © Bridget Curran 2008

Inspired Living, an imprint of
Allen & Unwin
83 Alexander Street
Crows Nest NSW 2065
Australia
Phone: (61 2) 8425 0100
Fax: (61 2) 9906 2218
Email: info@allenandunwin.com
Web: www.allenandunwin.com

Cataloguing-in-Publication details are available from the National Library of Australia
www.librariesaustralia.nla.gov.au

ISBN 978 1 74175 514 5

Internal design and illustrations by Zoë Sadokierski
Inside cover photograph: Pedro Almeida
Set in 12/13 pt Perpetua by Midland Typesetters, Australia
Printed in Australia by McPhersons Printing Group

10 9 8 7 6 5 4 3 2

Mixed Sources

Product group from well-managed
forests, and other controlled sources
www.fsc.org   Cert no. SGS-COC-004121
© 1996 Forest Stewardship Council

The paper in this book is FSC certified.
FSC promotes environmentally responsible,
socially beneficial and economically viable
management of the world's forests.

Nihil Obstat: Rev. Fr Brian G. O'Loughlin, JCD PhD
                 Vicar General

Imprimatur: +Barry James Hickey DD
                 Archbishop of Perth, WA

                 11 February 2008
                 Feast of Our Lady of Lourdes

The Nihil Obstat and Imprimatur are a declaration that a book is considered to be free from
doctrinal or moral error. It is not necessarily implied that those who have granted them agree
with the contents, opinions or statements expressed.

For Granny
Margaret Mary Phillips

Contents

Preface

Inever, ever, ever wanted to write a book about Mary. I've
never had a great devotion to her, quite the opposite. The
more devotion I saw Mary receive, the more critical I would
become. Many of my friends adored Mary and tried everything
to make me love her too. They argued with me, presenting
theological, intellectual arguments; they told me soft, romantic
stories and showed me sentimental images of her. Nothing
worked.

Well, that's not strictly true. I am a firm believer in the
power of prayer, and I think their prayer started to stir something within me. I couldn't escape the feeling that something
wasn't right. Either all these good people had misunderstood
Mary, or I had misunderstood her. I began to pray to God that
I would come to love Mary as much as he wanted me to.

I think this book is the answer to that prayer. When Maggie
Hamilton at Allen & Unwin rang me to talk about a 'Mary
book', I thought she was writing it herself. When she asked *me*
to write it, I was truly amazed. I tried to suggest other writers
who would be more suitable for the job. I felt that it should be
written by someone with a strong devotion to Mary. But it soon
became clear that this was something I had to do.

If I saw an apparition of Mary, I would think I was seeing
a ghost. If I heard her voice, I would think I was going crazy.
But if I spent many months reading, researching, writing,
praying and speaking to total strangers from all cultures, all
religions, all over the world, I might come to understand

Mary and love her in some way too. I always wanted to be a writer, and I love to listen to people's stories. Mary knows how to reach out to her children in ways that are meaningful and specific to them, and I'm convinced that through this book she has reached out to me.

Introduction
— Who Is Mary? —

She was a poor Jewish girl, engaged to an older man, Joseph. An angel appeared to her and asked her to bear the Son of God. She was amazed. She couldn't imagine how this could be possible, as she was a virgin. Yet she humbly consented. The angel assured her that all things are possible with God, and vanished.

Joseph knew the child couldn't be his. He was a compassionate, kind man and wanted to spare Mary the shame and scandal of a public divorce. So he decided to break their engagement privately. An angel appeared to him, telling him to put aside his concerns and take Mary as his wife. Joseph accepted this, and they were married. After Jesus was born, Mary was by his side for all the great and terrible events of her son's life. After his death and resurrection, she continued to live a life of humble faith until she passed away and was taken into heaven.

It's a strange story, and people have struggled to understand it for centuries. Stranger still are the many beautiful stories which emerged after Mary's death. Her presence on earth is still felt by people of many cultures and faiths. For those who have never been raised or schooled in any formal religion, Mary is still a figure of inexplicable attraction and consolation.

Even before Mary's birth, prophets spoke of a great and powerful virgin of humble origins who would give birth to the redeemer of mankind. That's not an easy figure to believe in, let alone understand or love.

No other woman in history can claim such a strange and

exalted role, and it seems incredible that such a person could have ever walked the earth. No one seems to have been more surprised about it than Mary herself. Everything we know of her points to Mary as a humble woman. She was a herald, a carer, and at once mother, daughter and spouse to God himself, yet in spite of all that—and in spite of her extraordinary, sometimes spectacular miracles, she's still very human.

Love gave her a thousand names.
—Flemish hymn on the many titles of Mary

Who *is* Mary, really? We have many beautiful names for her: 'Myrrh of the Sea', 'Light Giver', 'Enlightened One', 'Mother of the Lord'. How did a poor Jewish girl, Miryám the wife of Joseph and the mother of Jesus Christ, become 'Our Lady', 'Saint Mary', 'the Blessed Virgin', 'Holy Mother'?

It can take a lifetime to get to know Mary and the many ways she is loved. As these chapters unfold, my hope is that the reader will come to experience more of the beauty, power and gentle wisdom of Mary, and to understand why she means so much to so many.

This book is not a definitive account of the miracles of Mary, but rather a glimpse into who she is. Sometimes there are amazing similarities in stories which take place in different cultures, different times. Mary appears to us in many ways, through art and the written word, through apparitions, or sometimes as a presence or inspiration. Although the meaning of her message is not always clear, the motivation behind it is always love, the gentle, intense love of a mother for her children.

Mary of Matara
— Sri Lanka —

In the early morning of 26 December 2004, the seaside city of Matara, in Sri Lanka, was struck by a tsunami that claimed the lives of thousands of people. Father Charles Hewawasam was in the middle of a service when a woman at the back of the church began shouting. His first impulse was to ignore her. But then, through the window, he saw a van floating by. He scarcely had time to warn everyone before the modest church was flooded. The terrified parishioners fled to the second level of a nearby three-storey building.

The few chaotic moments that followed seemed like an eternity. As the waters began to recede, Father Charles raced to save the Host and a small, treasured statue of the Virgin Mary and the infant Jesus. But he was too late. The statue had been swept away. Father Charles remained where he stood, paralysed with the shock of this loss, until a woman called to him from the choir loft, telling him to save himself while there was still time. With a heavy heart, he turned and ran for the door. Already the waters had receded, leaving behind a 1.5-kilometre strip of sodden earth.

Without delay he rushed towards the parish house, where he had left his mother, family and friends. To his shock the entire building had been submerged. The only thing he could do now was rescue the wounded. Somehow he found the strength to drag the people he found into a newer building where many of his parishioners had taken refuge.

This was only the calm before the storm. Barely fifteen minutes after the first onslaught came a second, even more destructive, wave. Those who had taken shelter in the three-storey building watched in horror as their friends and neighbours were crushed under falling walls and debris or swept away. Then a third wave crashed over them. The terrible screams and desperate prayers were silenced by the roar of the rushing water.

Forty-five parishioners survived, including Father Charles' family and friends. A further twenty-three parishioners weren't so fortunate. Sister Bernadette Koolmeyer, who less than an hour earlier had been by Father Charles' side assisting at Mass, also died. All that Father Charles owned had been washed away. He had no money, no clothes, not even his cassock.

Adding to the tragedy of the tsunami was the loss of the parish's beloved Lady of Matara. All that remained was the small pedestal on which this lovely statue had stood for many years. As he stared in dismay at the empty pedestal, Father Charles was surprised to see that the glass which had protected the priceless statue was intact. It looked as if Mary had simply vanished. The statue's valuable jewellery was also missing. Almost a hundred years old, it had been used to decorate the statue during its annual festival celebrations.

Gloomily, Father Charles returned to his church with a group of helpers to assess the damage. On the road, he met a young man. Remarkably, there in his shoulder bag was the antique jewellery belonging to Our Lady of Matara. This was a wonderful sign, but the real miracle was yet to come.

The next few days were exhausting. Father Charles spent them finding bodies, identifying and burying the dead, consoling the parishioners. Every night he prayed for strength with a group of the faithful who gathered around an old picture of Our Lady of Matara found in the rubble in his room.

Then, early on the morning of 29 December, two men rushed into Father Charles' temporary home. 'Father!' they cried excitedly. 'We have found Our Mother of Matara.' Four hundred metres away, the statue had washed onto a sandy shore. Attracted by a glittering object among the trees, the caretaker of the land had found it.

The discovery was miraculous on so many levels. The tiny, fragile crown of the infant Jesus was intact. The hands, part of the foot and a gold chain were missing, but even those small pieces were soon found amid the rubble. The Lady of Matara had returned to the shores where she had first appeared many years ago.

Centuries before, a group of fishermen dragged in a huge crate from the ocean, caught in their nets off the coast of Matara. Inside was a small wooden statue of the Virgin Mary holding the child Jesus. Although they had been in the salt water for some time, both figures were unharmed. The statue was given to the parish priest of Matara.

Some years later, a cholera epidemic swept the land. Hundreds died. Desperate people of many faiths prayed to Our Lady of Matara and took her on a solemn procession among their disease-ravaged homes. Remarkably, within days the area was declared safe. There were no new cases of cholera, no further deaths. The Lady had saved her people.

Worn by centuries of tears, kisses and caresses from Mary's grateful devotees, the statue began to fade. In 1911 the local bishop, Joseph Van Reeth, decided to send it to Belgium for restoration. For the first time in 300 years, Our Lady of Matara left Sri Lankan shores. As befits Mary's title Star of the Sea, the statue travelled by ship. The repairs were successfully completed, but the ship carrying the statue home again was caught in two fierce storms and nearly ship-wrecked. Much of the cargo had to be thrown overboard, including the statue.

After a thorough search throughout Europe and Asia, the

statue was found in the possession of a man who refused to hand it over without a large payment. When his demands were refused, he smashed the face of the statue with a hammer and threw it away. It was recovered and sent back to Belgium for more repairs. After another tempestuous journey home, Our Lady of Matara settled in her parish in relative peace, until the tsunami.

Refuge in grief, Star of the Sea,
pray for the mourner, Oh, pray for me.
—CATHOLIC HYMN TO MARY, *HAIL, QUEEN OF HEAVEN*

Nestled on the shores of the Indian Ocean, Matara is not a large city. The Nilwala River winds through it, nourishing fields of rice, tea and spices. But the sea and fishing are also important to Matarans. It seems hardly surprising that in a town where water brings life and death, a patroness should have emerged from the waves, her history as changeable and unpredictable as the sea itself.

Little is known of the origins of the Lady of Matara, except that she is carved in a Portuguese style and is thought to be at least 300 years old. The tiny statue was hewn from a piece of ash—a wood associated in earlier times with the gods of ancient Europe and prediction of the weather. The ash was also connected with thunderstorms, which water and fertilise the earth. As a 'water' plant, the ash was believed to have command over the four elements. It could be used for protection, prosperity, prophecy, health, and rituals involving water and the sea. It is curious that Our Lady of Matara, crafted from a material long associated with water, came so mysteriously from the waves. What is most wonderful is that she is an important symbol of love, hope and healing to the local people, Buddhists, Muslims and Christians, in Matara.

The story of Our Lady of Matara reminds us of Mary's enduring care for human beings over several centuries, and in some of the most traumatic events imaginable. Mary always seems to be there for us, a strong yet gentle presence to those who know her, a more mysterious figure to those who do not.

Mary of Vailankanni
— India —

In ancient times, Vailankanni, in southern India, was a stop on the trade route to Rome and Greece. As time passed, its great history as a port city was forgotten. Today just a small town on the Bay of Bengal, it harbours a deep and ancient devotion.

On a warm, sunny day in the 16th century, a young Hindu shepherd boy was going about his daily business. As he walked down Anna Pillai Street on his way to deliver some buttermilk, he found the searing heat more oppressive than usual. Resting under a banyan tree beside a pond, the exhausted boy fell into a deep sleep. With a sudden strong gust of wind, he woke as a woman bathed in light appeared. She was holding a child. There was something about these two strangers that seemed unusual to him. Their faces shone softly with golden light. Smiling, the lady asked for some milk for her son.

The astonished boy leapt to his feet and offered the milk. Once the child had drunk his fill, he and his mother smiled in gratitude, and the shepherd boy happily continued on his way.

As he approached his destination, he had the sudden, terrible realisation that the milk he had given away was not his to give. It belonged to his customer, a wealthy landlord who was the sort of man it was unwise to displease. As the poor boy wondered what to do, he knew he must tell the man the truth.

By the time he reached the landlord's home, the man was angry. His milk was late. The boy explained why he had been delayed, apologising profusely for the missing milk. But as he and the landlord looked at the milk pot, they saw it was filling up. It filled right to the brim and began spilling out. Realising that it was no ordinary woman that the boy had encountered, the landlord set off with the boy to the pond. To their astonishment, the lady appeared once again. If any words were exchanged, they are lost to history. News of the incident soon spread. The excitement of the local people is still remembered, as they praised the strange, lovely woman. The pond became known as Matha Kulam, Our Lady's Pond.

Another young Vailankanni boy used to sell buttermilk as he lay in the low branches of a banyan tree. Crippled from birth, he lived with his widowed mother in great poverty, and would supplement their meagre income by begging. His mother would carry him to the banyan tree every morning, and pick him up at the end of the day.

One intensely hot day toward the close of the 16th century, the boy was startled by a sudden, bright light. At first he shouted for help. Then he saw a beautiful woman before him. She cradled an infant in her arms with the same tenderness with which his mother would carry him to the banyan tree. The child had an ethereal glow. Both mother and child wore dazzling white clothes. The woman smiled and sweetly asked for a cup of buttermilk for her child.

The boy felt an inexplicable joy as he handed her a cup and watched the child drink. Although he didn't know these strangers, it was like serving royalty. He was overwhelmed by their appreciation and love.

'I have chosen this place to favour my people,' the lady said. She then thanked the boy for his generosity and asked him to go to Nagapattinam, fifteen kilometres away, to visit a particular wealthy man. She wanted the boy to tell him all that had happened, and to ask him to build a chapel at Vailankanni in her honour.

With great sadness the boy explained that he couldn't help her, as he was a cripple. But the woman simply smiled and told him to walk.

The boy found himself scrambling to his feet and taking a few steps. Suddenly nothing seemed impossible. With excited leaps, he ran all the way to Nagapattinam, brimming with good health.

At Nagapattinam the boy's task was easy. Mary had visited the rich man in a dream the night before, instructing him to build a chapel in her honour. Now this breathless boy confirmed this mission. Together they went to the place of the boy's vision, where they helped build a small, thatched chapel in the lady's

. . . The feeling I had then has since been growing on me, that all this kneeling and prayer could not be mere superstition; the devout souls kneeling before the Virgin could not be worshipping mere marble. I have an impression that I felt then that by this worship they were not detracting from, but increasing, the glory of God.
—MAHATMA GANDHI, *MY EXPERIMENTS WITH TRUTH: AN AUTOBIOGRAPHY*

honour. Inside, a statue of the woman and her baby—whom they now knew were Mary and Jesus—was placed on the altar.

The local people were amazed at the miraculous healing of the lame boy. News of the story spread, and soon pilgrims of all faiths were flooding to the chapel, seeking peace and healing. Many more miracles were attributed to prayers before the statue of the Holy Mother and Child, which came to be known as Arokia Matha—Our Lady of Good Health.

The third great miracle of Vailankanni took place on its sandy shores a century later, when a Portuguese merchant vessel was caught in a violent storm while sailing from Macau to Ceylon. Furious winds hurled gigantic waves against the helpless ship. Everyone on board fell to their knees and cried to Mary, promising to build a church in her honour wherever they should land.

Suddenly there was silence. The winds ceased, the waves receded, and in no time the sea was calm. In awe and relief, the once terrified sailors coaxed their injured vessel to Vailankanni.

The fishermen of Vailankanni were surprised to see a clutch of battered, exhausted sailors on the beach, kneeling, crying, and praying. Recognising them as Christians, they guided the men to the simple, now very old chapel of Our Lady of Good Health.

There the men continued to give thanks for their lives. As the villagers told them about the miraculous origins of the shrine, they thanked God and Mary, and marvelled at the significance of the date that had brought them all together. It was 8 September, the feast of the birthday of the Virgin Mary.

Mindful of their vow, they set about building a brick church, with a great dome and European windows, on the site of the old thatched chapel. The day the new church was completed was a day of great celebration, as they dedicated the holy place to the nativity of the Virgin Mary. They would often return to the shrine bearing gifts from their travels all over the world. To this day porcelain plates from China depicting scenes from the Bible still adorn the altar of the great basilica.

Today people of all cultures and faiths flock to Vailankanni for the annual novena, a nine-day festival of prayer, in Mary's honour, to show their devotion to the Lady who brings hope and healing.

My Healing

A few years ago I began to have health problems. I was referred to a number of specialists, but no one knew what was wrong with me.

Finally I went to a haematologist, who said I had a rare blood disorder. At first, as I began to take medication, things went OK. But then my body seemed to go haywire. I was producing either too much or too little blood. My family was praying fervently for me and encouraging me to keep up my own prayers.

Then we were told about Our Lady of Vailankanni. My husband and I visited the shrine. The moment I entered the church, I felt an inner peace prompting me to surrender. I began to do just that. It was then that the healing process began.

It was as if the burden had been taken off me. I began to feel happy, energetic and positive. Since I returned from Vailankanni, my specialist has confirmed that my blood has stabilised. He told me that Our Lady has certainly looked after me. Now that I have gone through these difficulties, I pray for the sick every day. My husband and I have been back to Vailankanni to give thanks to Our Lady of Good Health, and we are planning to go again next year.

—Sandra, *Singapore*

Mary of Guadalupe
— Mexico —

A poor man walked along a familiar path through the rocky hills outside Tenochtitlán, Mexico. On a fine early December morning, just before dawn, the soft light of the sun was beginning to emerge on the horizon as he made his way to the city to attend church. He was barefoot and wore only a tilma, or poncho, coarsely woven from cactus fibres.

He had had a hard life, marrying and making a home on a small plot of land, where he laboured in the fields and wove mats. In his fifty-seven years he had witnessed the Spanish invasion of Mexico and its impact on his fellow native Americans. Intrigued by the faith of the Franciscan friars who settled nearby, he and his wife were among the first to be baptised. He took the name of Juan Diego. His wife did not live long after her baptism, so Juan Diego moved to his uncle's house to be closer to the church.

This day seemed like any other until the silence was broken by a strange, joyful song. As he came to the base of Tepeyac hill, Juan Diego found himself straining to catch the music. It was like a sweet, gentle chorus of many exotic birds. It was so hypnotic he almost felt as if he were dreaming.

The sound came from the east, and as he gazed in its direction it faded to silence. Then a voice echoed from the mountain above, calling him. Without hesitation Juan Diego climbed the short distance to the top of the hill, and saw before him the beaming figure of a beautiful Mexican girl, no more than fourteen years old. Although the sun had not yet fully risen, golden rays shone from her body. It was as though a great light glowed behind her. Light illuminated everything around her. The grey rocks, dry grasses and cacti were brought alive in colours that seemed almost translucent. The girl's beauty and nobility reminded him of an ancient Aztec princess.

Finally, she spoke to him. '*Xocoyte, Nopiltzin, campa tiauh?*' she asked him gently. 'Juan, smallest and dearest of my little children, where are you going?'

He was still in awe of this radiant figure. '*Xocoyata,*' he replied. 'My lady and my littlest daughter, I was hurrying to Tlaltelolco to see the Mass and hear the Gospel.'

As the Aztec beauty smiled back at him, she explained that she was the Virgin Mary and that she wanted a church to be built at this place, where she would show her compassion to her people and to all who sincerely asked her help. 'Here, I will see their tears; I will console them and they will be at ease. So run now to Tenochtitlán and tell the lord bishop all that you have seen and heard,' she told him.

The awestruck man fell on his knees before Mary, vowing to do as she asked. Rising, he left that holy site humbled by all he had experienced. As he set off in the direction of Tenochtitlán, today's Mexico City, the enormity of his task suddenly hit him. A church! To be built in the middle of nowhere, at the request of a poor old Indian. Even the trip would be a trial, as he had never been to the city before. He would have to walk many miles. It was a tough place. Indians were treated poorly by Spanish soldiers, not to mention any ruffians he might encounter. How could he find the bishop in such a large city, and convince him to follow Mary's request?

Juan Diego was a brave man and had great faith. He had made his promise, and so he walked to Tenochtitlán. Somehow he found his way to the door of the bishop's palace. After some manhandling and a very long wait, he was admitted into the presence of Don Fray Juan de Zumáraga, the bishop-elect, a man who was sympathetic to the Aztec Indians.

The bishop had many troubles of his own. Since the conquest of Mexico the king's administrators had violently oppressed the Aztec Indians. Bishop Zumáraga tried to alert the king, but he had no idea if his message had survived the long sea voyage to Spain. So he prayed to Mary, asking for guidance and a sign: Castilian roses from his native land.

Although the bishop listened carefully to Juan Diego's strange tale, he grew doubtful at the mention of a church in such a strange place. Having questioned Juan Diego, he explained that he would need to consider this request. The Indian could come back to discuss it again if he wished, but for now there was no more to be said on the matter. So Juan Diego took his leave and, dejected, made the lonely journey home.

Stopping at the hill where he had seen the beautiful Virgin Mary, he found her standing there, waiting for him. Kneeling, he poured out his heart to her. She listened intently as he told her he was not worthy to be her messenger. He begged her to choose someone else. At last, she spoke.

'Listen, little son,' she began. 'There are many I could send. But you are the one I have chosen for this task. So, tomorrow morning, go back to the bishop. Tell him it is the Virgin Mary who sends you, and repeat to him my great desire for a church in this place.'

Juan Diego was alarmed at the prospect of returning to the bishop's palace so soon, and admitted to the Virgin that he had grave fears of facing the same reception again. 'But I am your humble servant,' he added, 'And I willingly obey.'

With these words, he promised to return the next day. As was his custom, he rose before dawn for the long walk to church, then continued straight to Tenochtitlán. Eventually he reached the bishop's palace. Don Fray Juan de Zumáraga was not expecting to see the strange man again so soon. Juan Diego boldly told the bishop of his second encounter with Mary. He explained, too, that he had told her he was too lowly for such a task, but that she had insisted he return.

Don Fray Juan de Zumáraga questioned Juan Diego, and was impressed. The Indian seemed to be a simple man of great integrity. The bishop decided there was only one way to settle this matter. He left the room briefly and told some servants to follow Juan Diego discreetly and take note of any people he might speak with on his journey home. He then dismissed him.

The two servants returned with a disturbing report. Juan Diego had walked straight through the city without talking to anyone. He then continued for about 8 km at a brisk pace until he reached a small hill, where he suddenly disappeared. Though they searched the area, they found no sign of him.

Juan Diego had walked to the hill unaware that he was being followed. His only thought was of the Virgin Mary. He found her, as before, on the hilltop, and he knelt before her, telling her everything.

When she heard of the bishop's request for a sign, she seemed rather pleased. 'Very well, little son,' she smiled. 'Come back tomorrow at daybreak. I will give you a sign for him. You have taken much trouble on my account, and I shall reward you for it. Go in peace, and rest.'

There seemed little left for Juan Diego to do but go home. He returned to find his elderly uncle, Juan Bernardino, ill with a deadly fever. He spent the night and the next day nursing him, and missed his Monday appointment with Mary.

By Tuesday, Juan Bernardino's health had deteriorated, and it seemed certain he would pass away by nightfall. There was nothing more Juan Diego could do. His uncle needed a priest to administer the Last Rites, and at the old man's insistence Juan Diego ran to Tlaltelolco to fetch one.

The path took Juan Diego past the hill where he had seen the Lady. Embarrassed, he tried an alternative route around the hill, to avoid seeing her. But he met her on his path, and she asked him what was wrong.

With breathless anxiety he told her about his uncle's illness and this last great errand of mercy in search of a priest. He also begged her forgiveness for failing to meet her when he had promised to take a miraculous sign to the bishop. Mary listened with compassion, telling him not be afraid and promising to heal his uncle so he could accomplish the mission she had set for him.

'Go to the top of the hill,' she instructed, 'and cut the flowers that are growing there. Then bring them to me.' This must have seemed to Juan Diego a rather mundane errand when there were such important matters to attend to. Besides, at that time of year there was often frost on the hilltop, and no flowers could possibly be blooming there.

But Juan Diego found enough faith to obey. Climbing the hill, he was amazed to see fresh roses. Gathering up the flowers into his poor, rough tilma, he ran back to Mary. Taking the roses, she tenderly rearranged them in his tilma, considering each blossom carefully as she did so. When she had everything just right, she tied the corners of Don Juan's tilma behind his neck so nothing would fall out.

She gave him strict instructions not to show anyone but the bishop what he was carrying. Juan Diego was to explain the whole encounter, and how Mary had healed his uncle and arranged the flowers. Mary's final words were simple and encouraging. 'Remember, little son, that you are my trusted ambassador, and this time the bishop will believe all that you tell him.'

With these parting words, Juan Diego took the long path once again, the sweet fragrance of roses his only companion. Once he reached the palace, curious servants pushed Juan

Diego around and peered inside his tilma. But every time they tried to touch the roses, they took on the appearance of a painting or embroidery on the rough cloth. The hubbub brought the visitor to the bishop's attention.

Juan Diego was forced to break the rules of etiquette by remaining standing for fear of dropping a rose. He told the story of his third strange encounter with the Lady, then raising his hands, untied the knot. Fresh Castilian roses immediately fell in a heap on the floor, their delicate petals filling the room with the sweetest perfume. As amazing as the flowers were, all attention shifted away from them to Juan Diego.

The bishop's household fell to their knees. Imprinted on the weave of his tilma was an image of the blessed Virgin as Juan Diego remembered her—a beautiful Aztec woman, young, humble, but radiating a quiet dignity and deep, all-embracing love.

While the whole household wondered at the tilma, the bishop gazed at the roses. His personal prayer to Mary had been answered. He stood up in silence, gently took the tilma off Juan Diego, and placed it on a wall beside the altar in his private chapel. There, Juan Diego was able to kneel in reverence with the others, marvelling at the sign Mary had created.

For the next day and night Juan Diego remained a guest in the palace. His tilma was taken in triumphant procession to the cathedral, so all could pray before the sacred image. Then he took the bishop to the hilltop where Mary had directed him. She wasn't there. But there was no question of what was to be done now. Mary's church was to be built on that very spot.

His mission accomplished, Juan Diego returned home to his elderly uncle, who greeted him at the door with an amazing tale of his own.

Left alone and gravely ill, Juan Bernardino despaired of living another day. Then, in a moment of great desolation, a gentle white light had filled the room and a beautiful young woman appeared by his side. Enraptured by her very presence, he felt deeply peaceful. She promised he would be healed, and somehow he knew she spoke the truth. She explained that she had asked his nephew to go to the bishop with a picture of her that was to be enshrined at Tepeyac. 'Call me, and my image, Santa María de Guadalupe,' she then told him, and with these words she vanished, leaving the old man to bask in the light of the approaching dawn. He had been healed.

Juan Diego lived a further seventeen years after his encounters with Mary, in a small room attached to the church he had worked so hard to secure for the Lady. Here he welcomed all guests as the official custodian of the tilma. He would tell travellers his story and answer all questions patiently. He died peacefully in 1548, finally taken back into the arms of his loving mother of Guadalupe.

The symbolic meaning of the images on Juan Diego's tilma was particularly significant to the overwhelmingly pagan and illiterate natives of Mexico. By standing in front of the sun, Mary demonstrated her superiority over their sun god, Huitzilopochtli. By standing over the moon's crescent, she demonstrated her superiority over their moon god, Tezcatlipocha. But her humble, bowed head and praying hands suggested that she too knelt before someone greater. The black cross at her throat indicated her son, Jesus Christ. The sight of the image of the Lady of Guadalupe was enough to transform the hearts of an entire nation, and many converted instantly. The worn tilma of a Mexican peasant had succeeded where all the fiery sermons of Spanish missionaries had failed. Within seven years of the miracle, an estimated eight million Mexicans were converted to Christianity. To this day, Mexico has a profound devotion to Mary.

God of power and mercy,
you blessed the Americas at Tepeyac
with the presence of the Virgin Mary of Guadalupe.
May her prayers help all men and women
to accept each other as brothers and sisters.

Through your justice, present in our hearts
may your peace reign in the world.
—Opening prayer of the memorial of
Our Lady of Guadalupe

In the 20th century, scientific advances allowed the faithful a glimpse into the eyes of Mary. While examining some photographic images of Our Lady of Guadalupe in 1929, Alphonso Marcue Gonzales noticed something strange. Looking closely into her eyes, he saw the unmistakable figure of a man, one with a bearded face and a partial halo—a match with contemporary accounts of Juan Diego.

Doctors and optometrists have confirmed that the figure is there, and further suggested that Mary's eyes reflect light rays in the same way that human eyes reflect light under examination. Could it be that her final, loving gaze at Juan Diego was preserved forever?

Science has only emphasised the image's miraculous qualities. X-ray tests, infrared radiation photographs and art experts have confirmed that the flimsy cactus cloth, which is highly unsuitable as a painting canvas, has well outlived the twenty-year lifespan it would normally have had before disintegrating. Even to this day, it shows no signs of any sketching beneath it or paint strokes over it. Oil, tempera, water colour and fresco seem to be the four main media used to create different parts of the image. Exactly how it was applied, and how it survived with no signs of fading or damage for over 400 years, remains a mystery.

Devotees have painted other images on the tilma, on or near Our Lady of Guadalupe, but they have proved easy to distinguish from the original. 'Embellishments' on the image have faded over time, yet it seems the original figure has not. The golden border, the stars and the embroidery have never faded, so many consider them to be part of the original miraculous image. It has been close to destruction twice: first, when a cleaner accidentally spilt nitric acid on it, and again in

1921, when a bomb hidden in a bouquet of flowers was left at the church altar. The metal altar crucifix was left twisted, the stained glass and marble in the church shattered, but the tilma and its glass case remained unharmed. The twisted crucifix is still on display in the church, a testimony to the explosive force that was no match for the strength of the Lady of Guadalupe.

Mary of Walsingham
— England —

Once, England was a nation so devoted to Mary that it was widely known as 'Mary's dowry'. At its heart lay the humble medieval village of Walsingham—'England's Nazareth', a centre of pilgrimage.

Like life, undertaking a pilgrimage is not easy, but it can be deeply rewarding. Some believe that certain holy sites draw people, as places where heaven meets earth and the divine becomes almost tangible.

In the 11th century, Walsingham was a wealthy village located between Norwich and King's Lynn. Here the Saxon noblewoman Richeldis de Faverches was married to the lord of Walsingham Parva. They had one son, Geoffrey. Richeldis was widowed young and became a local philanthropist, generous to all around her. She had a deep love of Mary, and taught her son to love Mary, too. He eventually went on to fight in the Crusades, realising his dream of seeing Mary's original home in Nazareth.

Mary often brings comfort to her people in preparation for times of trial, and the Norman conquest of England was not far in the future when Richeldis received an extraordinary vision from Mary. Walsingham, she was told, would become a place of contemplation and miracles long after the invasion of England.

Richeldis was taken in spirit to Nazareth, where Mary asked her to build in Walsingham a replica of her home—the same house where the Archangel Gabriel had appeared to her, asking her to become the mother of God.

'Whoever seeks my help there will never go away empty-handed,' Mary promised. 'To all those who come to this place I will give my help.'

Obedient to Mary's request, Richeldis began to make plans. She had taken the house's measurements but was still unsure about the replica's exact location in Walsingham. She chose a site, but the first day of construction was plagued with problems. A fretful Richeldis spent much of that night in prayer, and when she finally fell asleep she awoke to the sound of an unearthly choir. It seemed to be coming from her garden. Curious, she followed the voices, and was amazed to find the house fully built about 200 metres from the site where the building work had begun. When the carpenters arrived they were amazed to find that the newly completed house was of the finest quality. It was assumed angels had done the work.

Made from wood, wattle and daub, the house was striking in its simplicity. Inside, a wooden statue of an enthroned Madonna and Child was said to have miraculously appeared. News of this holy shrine spread far and wide, and it soon became a popular place of pilgrimage.

Years later, Richeldis' son Geoffrey left a will bearing instructions for the building of a priory in Walsingham to protect the 'Holy House', as the shine was called. In the 14th century a chapel dedicated to Saint Catherine of Alexandria was built a mile from the priory as the last stop for pilgrims. It was known as the Slipper Chapel, because they would leave their shoes there and walk barefoot to the Holy House, the final 'holy mile' of their journey.

The house stood on the site of a well whose waters led to many miraculous cures. Almost four centuries later, in 1513, the visiting Dutch scholar Erasmus reported that this special water was 'efficacious in curing pains of the head and stomach'. Close to the Norfolk coast, Mary of Walsingham became known as the Virgin by the Sea, a comforter and guide to seafarers everywhere.

Writing in 1479, William of Worcester records that the house was just over seven by four metres. Great conversions, healings and answered prayers seemed to flow from it. The legend of Walsingham grew and was enshrined in ballads and literature. The earliest known story of the shrine is the 15th-century Walsingham Ballad, recited by pilgrims. Sir Walter Raleigh, Chaucer and even Shakespeare made references to Walsingham. In its heyday, it was a pilgrimage site, in the same class as Jerusalem and Rome. Its visitors included King David of Scotland, Richard II, Queen Anne, Queen Isabella of France, Robert the Bruce of Scotland, Catherine of Aragon and Anne Boleyn.

Edward I was said to have experienced a miracle there, when he was saved from a piece of falling masonry. Even Henry VIII visited many times, although it was his reformation that would lead to the destruction of the shrine and the burning of the statue of Mary in the 16th century. In spite of this he was said to have maintained his strong devotion to her until his death.

During this time, Walsingham's Augustinian community was closed and its wealth taken to London. Many holy images, including the statue of Mary, were subsequently destroyed or burned. Eleven people, including the sub-prior, were hanged, drawn and quartered outside the gates of the priory, and the home of prayer and contemplation was left in ruins. Over the years, the Slipper Chapel became a barn, a forge, a poor house, a cow byre and a workhouse. The king sold this priceless land for just £90. The many pilgrims who had venerated Mary with such devotion were devastated to have lost this holy place. Too frightened to revere Mary openly, English Catholics seemed to have had little choice but to try to forget the precious little shrine that had been England's Nazareth.

Walsingham was a very different place by the late 19th century. Charlotte Pearson Boyd, a wealthy Anglican, wanted to rekindle some of the spirit of Mary that Walsingham had lost. Like Richeldis centuries before, Charlotte had a deep faith that inspired her to do good works, managing an orphanage and caring for several religious orders. One day she realised that an old barn at Houghton St Giles bore a strong resemblance to a medieval church. Research revealed that this barn was nothing less than the Slipper Chapel. Remarkably, it had never been completely abandoned. Rumour suggested that people had continued to pray there illicitly even after it was desecrated.

Charlotte purchased the building, and work soon began on restoring the chapel that had once welcomed so many weary pilgrims. While it underwent restoration, Charlotte underwent a spiritual transformation and became a Catholic.

In the late 19th century Pope Leo XIII formally reinstated the old shrine of Our Lady of Walsingham in King's Lynn, 40 km from Walsingham, and the first pilgrimage since the Reformation was finally conducted, to the village itself, passing through the Slipper Chapel once again.

Reconciliation and a movement towards Mary came from Father Alfred Hope Patten. An Anglican priest, he has been largely credited with reestablishing the shrine in Walsingham. He had a new image carved, based on an old priory seal he had seen in the British Museum. From all the destruction of the Reformation, it was the only image of Our Lady of Walsingham to have survived.

Anglicans have a long and complicated history of Marian devotion, for some fear that reverence for Mary could turn into idolatry. But those who knew Father Patten say that he saw in Mary the loving face of a mother turned expectantly in hope of reconciliation among her children.

He received considerable criticism, but the reinstatement of Our Lady of Walsingham was overall a great success. 'I had an image of Our Lady carved,' the priest said, 'and God did the rest.'

So many people made pilgrimages to Walsingham that a larger church had to be built around the shrine. While it was being constructed, a natural spring was discovered which pilgrims from all over the world still visit today.

At the end of World War II, the US armed forces held the first Mass for many centuries in the ruins of the priory, in thanksgiving for victory.

In 1982, when Pope John Paul II visited London and celebrated Mass at Wembley Stadium, the image of Our Lady of Walsingham was placed at the altar by the directors of the Catholic and Anglican shrines. That simple but powerful gesture of devotion to Mary has led to renewed collaboration, dialogue and shared prayer. The Church replaced the feast of Our Lady of Ransom with the 24 September feast of Our Lady of Walsingham. Our Lady of Ransom was a title that had been given to Mary at a time when devotion to Mary was frowned upon, if not denounced. When Mary was recognised once more as Our Lady of Walsingham, it was the answer to centuries of prayer for England to be restored to Mary.

Today the world is full of Walsinghams, from Ontario, Canada, to Canterbury, New Zealand. There is even a Walsingham House School in Bombay, India. And just as Mary travelled to England all those centuries ago, so she continues today to reach out to those who seek her.

In 2007, several large areas of Walsingham were flooded, including the Holy Mile pilgrimage route. During this deluge the route was impassable by car. The only way to reach the shrine was the old-fashioned pilgrim's way—by foot. Remarkably the shrine was undamaged.

As England's only shrine to Mary, Walsingham continues to draw thousands of visitors each year. As well as the
Anglican and Catholic shrines, there is a former Methodist
chapel turned Russian Orthodox church. Visitors still speak
of a 'powerful and prayerful presence', even amongst the
priory ruins and the remnants of the holy wells. After religious turmoil, Mary has enabled Walsingham to flourish
once more and, out of the ashes of a painful past, England's
Nazareth has emerged as a centre for deepening spirituality
and reconciliation.

Mary at Nazareth, pray for all families.
Mary, model of womanhood, pray for all women.
Woman of humility, keep us in mind.
Alone of all women, mother and virgin,
Mother most happy, virgin most pure.
  —From the Litany to Our Lady of Walsingham

Drawn to Mary

It was a picture of Our Lady of Walsingham that led me to the adver-
tisement for my job as education officer at the Anglican shrine in
Walsingham. Ever since, this image has been very special to me. I cannot
describe it really, but when I enter the Holy House in our church here
and look up at the image, I feel drawn to Mary as one who understands
all that women go through. In bad times I can stand before Our Lady
and release all that is on my mind.

Many pilgrims to Walsingham describe this experience as 'coming
home', for of course the house represents the place where Mary's life was
turned upside-down at the Annunciation, and also the home where she
and Joseph brought up Jesus.

I spend my working life trying to bring alive to children the
power of place—holy space. No matter how distant the original
legend is, we keep asking ourselves, is there something powerful about
this place?

I'm an Anglican, and I've been working at the shrine here for
eleven years now. One devotion we have is the Sprinkling at the Well, the
Saxon well found when the church was being built back in the 1930s.

People receive the water on a spoon and are blessed with the sign of the cross as it is poured over their hands. These are symbols of refreshment, their baptism, and Jesus' love for them. In this simple devotion they let go and offer up all the burdens that they, or someone they love, are carrying. They pray for healing. Many describe profound healing. It's often not anything too dramatic, but sometimes it is. I remember a lady several years ago whose sight returned.

Lots of tourists, who often latch onto school groups, have told me they have been profoundly affected by coming here. A couple turned up with a terminally ill baby one day and asked for baptism. One of our priests baptised the child. It was very moving. They had heard about us on the radio and driven all the way from London. Seeing their release of all their pain here was very moving. The child later died.

I hear many pilgrims' stories about how, in times of need, this place has been a stronghold for them. I remember an old lady who was kneeling in the Holy House one day for hours when I had school kids in. She later said she comes every year on pilgrimage and it's like coming home to her, as near to the home of Jesus as she can get. The kids were really touched by her faith, and by her simple desire to pray in there.

Lots of youngsters who take part in our youth pilgrimage are so affected by their experience here. They feel the vibrancy of the place and of all our worship. Many say it really helps them face the difficulties of being a young Christian. It's a neutral place where they can just relax and be. This place acts like a sponge, taking in everyone's needs, anxieties and joys and holding them up to God. No demands are made on people. I think that's the wonder of a holy place. Listeners are available to hear their stories and help link them in with God's story.

When my son was seven he was in a wheelchair with arthritis, and he asked to come to the well. I was sceptical. He received the water and afterwards said, 'I still hurt, Mummy, but I feel better inside.' I think that sums up what places like this are about.

Coming to an unfamiliar place and yet receiving these gifts, being listened to, being cared for, and spending time in prayer, is so helpful for so many.

—Janet, *Walsingham, England*

In the Steps of Great-Grandfather

When I was a seminarian, way back in the 1950s, I spent some holiday time with my great-great-aunt at Tocumwal, on the banks of the Murray River in New South Wales. She possessed some of the books of my great-grandfather, who had died in 1896. Among them was a prayer book called Garden of the Soul, *a popular substitute for a Sunday missal in those days.*

In the rear of the book was a small letter, dated, if I remember correctly, 1848. In it my great-grandfather told his parents that he believed he had little future to look forward to in England, his homeland. He had decided to emigrate to Australia.

His parents encouraged him to make a journey to the shrine of 'the Lady' (as he termed the Blessed Virgin Mary) at Walsingham, Norfolk, to seek her help and guidance at the chapel—the former Slipper Chapel. He wrote that the chapel was a barn, and some distance from the centre of the old priory ruins. Both his parents had made the pilgrimage at a time when there was no Catholic activity around the ruins of the old shrine in Walsingham.

My great-great-aunt died, and no one knows what happened to the old prayer book. I did rescue several other old books from the library, but retain only a memory of that prayer book. It was enough to encourage me to follow in my great-grandfather's footsteps, and seek Our Lady of Walsingham's blessings and prayers for my family, as he had done so long ago.

I visited the holy places a number of times over the next couple of days as I spent quiet time at the several churches and the old abbey site. A very kind lady in the Catholic shop by the chapel kindly gave me a statue of Our Lady of Walsingham. I have it near me as I write this.

I also called in at another shop where several Catholics collected contributions from pilgrims for good works among the poor around the world. The lady behind the counter was sister to a former parishioner of mine. We exchanged news, views, and lots of good cheer. It was all very memorable.

And what was I thinking when I came to the Slipper Chapel? Well, I noted how tidy, clean, and quietly inspiring it was. It must have looked rather different when it was a barn. The Church of Reconciliation next door was a modern and less notable place, but it too was a place of prayer and worship. Pilgrims and tourists came and went all the time I was there.

I tried to imagine what my great-grandfather might have been thinking. This was a holy place, and centre of honour for 'the Lady', as he called Our Lady. I stood there and said my rosary, thanking her for the favours and blessings he had sought so long ago, and which had been granted to my family over the next 150 years. I thanked my great-grandfather for his devotion, and for handing on the faith of our forebears to generations now thoroughly Australian.

Then I visited the chapel itself. I suppose he was not able to do that. And I reckon he would have walked the mile to the ruined site of the old abbey destroyed by the king's men four centuries ago. It is such a peaceful place—beautiful and graced. I thought he must have noticed the attraction and holiness of the place even then. That is all there now is to the story—but I still hold it as a blessed memory.

—Bishop Hilton Deakin, *Victoria*

Mary of Le Puy
— France —

Le Puy-en-Velay is the site of one of the oldest shrines of Mary in Europe. A woman, plagued by a mysterious fever, came to Mont Anis in the hope of being cured. The hill had a strong reputation as a powerful and ancient place of healing. Mary appeared, and asked the woman to build a chapel there. A second woman was also healed on the hill, and she too saw an apparition of Mary requesting a chapel. The chapel was eventually constructed, but not consecrated. When a bishop finally arrived to conduct the consecration, he found the chapel shimmering with light and music. He was convinced the chapel had already been blessed by angels.

Legend records a devotion to Mary that even preceded her birth: veneration of a black Madonna reportedly carved by the prophet Jeremiah. Another story suggests that when St Louis, King of France, had been captured by Moors during the Crusades, he so impressed their leader that he was given a cedar statue of Mary as a gift. The statue, once venerated by Muslims, was then brought to Le Puy, where great kings, saints and popes came to pray. At its peak it was one of the most popular shrines in Europe. During the French Revolution, the statue that was once venerated by the Emperor Charlemagne was ridiculed in a mock trial, then guillotined and burned.

A new, black marble replica has since replaced the original black Madonna, and with it came renewed devotion to Mary. A large 19th-century statue of Notre Dame de France (Our Lady of France) dominates the skyline of Le Puy. It is made from the metal of 213 cannons.

From the weapons of war, a tower of peace.

You who carry in your heart a bothering worry,
pain, great joy,
you who need God's strength,
God's light,
God's help.
Talk about it to Mary,
her son, Jesus
and the flame of this candle
will prolong your prayer.
—PRAYER FROM LE CHEMIN DU PUY-EN-VELAY

Weeping Icon in Transylvania

Among the most holy treasures that have enlightened the life of Orthodox Christians in Transylvania is the holy icon of the Mother of God from the Romanian Orthodox Nicula Monastery. Around this icon have gathered, as bastions of freedom and peace, generations and generations of Romanian Orthodox Christians. For more than three centuries, this most venerated icon has brought comfort and support to many shattered souls who prayed before it.

The history of the holy relic begins in 1681 with a priest who painted icons for the faithful. After a few years this particular icon was bought from the priest by a peasant and given to the church in Nicula. On 15 February 1694, a few Austrian officers came into the church, and while they were admiring the icon they saw it was weeping . . . real tears were coming out of the eyes of the Holy Mother of God. They ran and brought the priest and all the villagers, and they all saw the tears that were falling on the ground. The holy icon kept weeping for twenty-six days; people would come and wipe the tears. Many sick people came and touched the tears and were healed, and it was said that no one who saw the holy icon died a violent death.

After many years the icon was taken by a Hungarian count to his castle, but the Romanian peasants asked for it back and threatened to burn the castle if the icon was not returned. The emperor in Vienna decided that the icon would be put in a new church which would be a part of a monastery, to be built by the count close to Nicula village. The count built the church on the hills above Nicula and put the icon there.

In 1948, when the communists came to power in Romania, the Romanian Orthodox Church was persecuted, priests were imprisoned, churches were burned to ashes and people were forbidden to pray or attend holy services. The monks from Nicula were scared that the icon *would be taken away from them again, so they hid it in a small village near the monastery. It remained there for almost twenty years, until the authorities finally found out about it. Bishop Teofil of Cluj took it away and brought it to the chapel of the Orthodox Theological Seminary of Cluj, where it stayed for many years. On 24 March 1992, in an incredible pilgrimage, the icon was taken back to the monastery of Nicula. Everyone walked more than 30 miles (42 km) to get to the monastery, singing hymns to the Theotokos, the Mother of God, all the way to the monastery. Every year on 15 August, hundreds of thousands of Orthodox Christians gather at the Monastery of Nicula to praise the icon and venerate the Holy Mother of God. Throughout the centuries, the icon has made many miracles for those who came to ask for help and guidance.*

For me, going on the pilgrimage to the Monastery of Nicula is the most moving moment of the year. Everywhere you look, there are people praising and singing, everyone's eyes are glowing with joy. Earth is united with heaven in prayer. Glory be to God for all things!

—Father Marius, *Romania*

IMAGES OF LOVE

An icon—Greek for picture—is an image, usually a painting, created in and for prayer. It is carefully copied in an established style, just as manuscripts were copied by hand before printing was invented. Legend has it that Christ's disciple Saint Luke the Evangelist painted the very first icons. There are many recorded stories of miraculous icons from all over the world.

Self-expression and improvisation are frowned upon in iconography. Icons are invariably unsigned, as an act of humility on the part of the artist. The emphasis is on the holy subject rather than the mere instrument that attempts to reproduce it. The point of iconography is to create the most accurate copies possible, capturing as much of the spirit of the original as possible. The effort to replicate every detail of an icon requires great concentration, and this induces deep contemplation. Art becomes a prayer.

Icons are part of the Christian Orthodox tradition. They often represent saints or angels, but one of the most beloved subjects is Mary. She is depicted in many roles, as a prayerful mother, a guide, a loving and forgiving mother, and as an intercessor who prays for those who seek her aid.

Mary, Kazanskaya
— Russia —

The icon type known as Hodigitria—literally, She who shows the way—is a sombre but beautiful image. Mary holds the infant Jesus, pointing towards him. Their faces are serious; their heads do not touch. Mary is simply indicating the path to holiness in the person of her son. It is an ancient type, attributed, like many icons, to the evangelist Luke.

The Theotokos (Mother of God) or Kazanskaya, is a close-up variation of this icon style, and features the infant Jesus standing. Copies of this icon are often small, a little larger than a sheet of A4 paper, and are traditionally given as wedding gifts to be displayed in a place of honour inside the couple's home.

The original icon was said to have arrived in Russia from Constantinople in the 13th century. In the chaos of a Tartar siege two centuries later, it was lost.

A fire destroyed Kazan in the 16th century. In the aftermath of the disaster, Mary appeared in a dream to a nine-year-old girl called Matrona. She told the child precisely where to recover the icon, and instructed her to go and see the archbishop. The little girl felt daunted by the task. But Mary gently persisted, and appeared to Matrona again in two more dreams. Finally she obeyed, and a group of people assembled to begin the excavation. They had little success.

Then Matrona was handed a shovel. Beneath the rubble she unearthed the holy Lady of Kazan. Wrapped in a red cloth and buried under the ashes of a house, she still glowed with all the beauty of a newly made icon.

The people suspected that the icon had been buried for protection from the invading Tartars all those years before. In this time of need for Kazan, Our Lady had chosen to make herself known again. The archbishop reverently took the icon to the Church of Saint Nicholas. On that same day, a blind man was cured at the church. Many miracles were attributed to the Lady and great feasts were held in her honour.

Our Lady of Kazan also became renowned for miracles. Prayer and the icon were credited with saving Russia three times, from Polish, Swedish and Napoleonic invasions. At the height of the icon's popularity it would be carried in solemn liturgical processions through city streets and along city walls, so everyone could revere Mary and pray for her protection for their community.

Several copies of the icon were made, and all had miracles attributed to them. One icon, stolen from a cathedral in Kazan in 1904, was widely believed to have been the original. It was adorned with gold and jewels, and when the thieves were captured they claimed they had slashed and burned it. People saw the icon's destruction as a bad omen. Within two decades came World War I and the Russian Revolution. Kazanskaya was believed to particularly protect the Romanov dynasty, which perished in the revolution.

One icon of Our Lady of Kazan was kept in a great basilica in Moscow. During the revolution it was spirited away unharmed, but the basilica was destroyed. The date was 13 October 1917. On that same day, in Fátima, on the other side of Europe, Mary appeared to a group of peasant children to warn them of the impending errors of Russia and its future conversion.

During World War II, the Nazis laid siege to Leningrad (St Petersburg) for 900 days. During the siege, an icon of Our Lady of Kazan appeared and was led in procession around the fortifications of the city, only to disappear into obscurity. Another

Kazan icon was enshrined in Fátima in the 1970s and later given to Pope John Paul II. He kept it in his study for eleven years. 'It has been by my side,' he said, 'and accompanied me with a maternal gaze in my daily service to the Church.'

The Pope wanted to return Kazanskaya to Russia, so after a period of public veneration at St Peter's Basilica in Rome, the icon was delivered to Moscow as an unconditional gift to the Russian Church. On the icon's next feast day, Patriarch Alexis II and Mintimer Shaymiev, President of Tatarstan, enshrined the icon at the Annunciation Cathedral of the Kazan Kremlin.

Finally the holy icon of Kazan had come home again.

O people, let us run to that quiet good haven, to the speedy helper, the warm salvation, to the Virgin's protection. Let us speed to prayer and hasten to repentance. For the Mother of God pours out her mercy, anticipates needs, and averts disasters for her patient and God-fearing servants.

—Orthodox hymn

The Grand Duchess and the Holy Queen

The Grand Duchess Olga Romanov, eldest daughter of Tsar Nicholas II and Tsarina Alexandra of Russia, was a 'hot tempered' but affectionate young princess. Olga was also a deeply contemplative, poetic soul.

With tensions running high in Russia, the tsar was forced to abdicate. But it was not enough to hold back the full onslaught of the Bolshevik revolution. Olga and her parents, brother and sisters were rounded up and imprisoned in Ipatiev House. No one could see in or out.

In 1917, Olga, her family and several servants were executed in the cellar of Ipatiev House. It was not until after her brutal murder that many of Olga's writings were discovered. These writings, mostly poems and prayers, show the sensitivity and spirituality of a young girl with a great devotion to Mary.

At the back of an icon of the Virgin Mary, a prayer was discovered, believed to have been written by Olga and hidden from the gaze of her jailors. It talks of her fears for herself and her family, and her unwavering faith in Mary.

Today, the Russian Orthodox Church recognises Olga and her family as saints. An Orthodox cathedral has been built on the site of Ipatiev House. The duchess who humbly called Mary her 'Tsarina and Queen' is now venerated herself as the Holy Royal Martyr Grand Duchess Olga.

The Convent That Would Not Burn

Our convent of Our Lady of Kazan is nestled in the quiet bushland of Campbelltown, on the western edge of Sydney. The countryside is beautiful, but unfortunately prone to bushfires.

One such bushfire threatened us some years ago, in 1990. The flames raced through the dry grass and trees, heading along the gully towards our convent. There is a school beside us, and we phoned to warn the teachers. As the school was evacuated, we turned to prayer, and thought of the Icon of the Burning Bush. This is an icon of the Virgin Mary pointing the way to Jesus. Its name refers to the burning bush that Moses discovered after fleeing Egypt. God spoke to him from the bush, warning Moses that he stood on holy ground. Theotokos [the Virgin Mary] is very like the burning bush. Just as it was consumed by fire but did not burn, so the Virgin Mary gave birth to Christ and yet retained her purity.

Hoping to be saved from the approaching flames, we turned to this holy icon. Our mother superior, Abbess Evpraksia, carried Our Holy Mother, while Sister Ambrosia and I walked on each side of her, praying and singing hymns in honour of the icon of the Holy Mother of God. Mother Superior walked around the entire border of the convent, holding Our Lady in her arms. Finally we returned to the eastern fence, where the flames had now reached a height of five metres. I will never forget those tremendous flames. Mother Superior boldly raised the holy icon high above her head, and with a great sign of the cross, she blessed the approaching fire.

It stopped immediately. It seemed as though the flames were somehow pressed down, low to the ground as if bowing. Then they vanished.

In the ensuing calm a neighbour of ours approached, amazed. He was a Russian immigrant, though he had long ceased to believe in miracles and the divine. When he saw the holy icon defeat the great flames, his heart melted and he praised God. It was truly a great miracle.

—Abbess Maria, *New South Wales*

THE MIRACLE AT NEW NORCIA MISSION

New Norcia is Australia's only monastic town, established by Benedictine monks in 1846. In an account recorded in his diaries in 1847, Bishop Rosendo Salvado describes a miraculous story of faith and its effects in uniting two cultures in a common devotion to Mary.

'. . . we saw that a terrible fire was burning the bush around the mission, and was getting close to our half-reaped crop. Immediately, natives and all, we ran to stop the fire from spreading, only to find ourselves helpless against a mass of flame and smoke that enveloped the tallest trees over a front of about a mile. Doing what we could, we took up positions to beat the three-foot-high grass, which had already caught fire and which stretched the whole way between our property and the bushfire, and we used for this purpose green branches, as the natives do.

'But the fire raced on, helped by a strong wind, scorching our hands and faces, singeing our hair and beards and clothes, and making us despair of bringing it under control. In this extremity, when it became evident that all our property—the whole result of our toil and sweat—was going to be destroyed, we had recourse to the mercy of God, invoking the intercession of the Holy Virgin as our special Protectress. We brought out a picture of our Blessed Lady which had the place of honour on our poor altar, and took it to the corner of the field nearest the flames, leaving it leaning against the wheat-stalks that were due to catch fire within a few minutes.

'We prayed at the same time that our Protectress would cast a glance of pity on us, and on the poor natives. Through the greatness of God an unexpected portent occurred. Scarcely had the sacred picture been placed facing the flames than the wind suddenly changed direction and drove the flames back to the part already burnt, and with this the danger ended.

'A large number of natives witnessed this marvellous event. Some of them, looking at the miraculous picture, uttered these words with simplicity and truth: *Jaco Uilar tenga cumbar! Baal penin, caia baal mekan; n-alla tonga but.* (This white lady knows so much! It was she who did it, yes, it was she! We can't do things like that.)

'In thanksgiving for the heavenly favour we had been granted, we offered a solemn votive Mass of the Mother of God next morning, at which many of the natives were present. The event became famous; every strange native who came to our mission was informed in detail by the local ones about what happened, and then taken to the chapel to be shown the White Lady who knew and could do so much.'

The Virgin of the Snakes
— Greece —

The feast of the Dormition is the day Mary fell asleep for the last time. On the island of Kefalonia, it is a day marked by the strange appearance of small snakes. They are considered harmless, and in fact their appearance is thought to signify good fortune. The distinctive dark snakes also bear small crosses on their faces. They crawl through the Church Panayia of Langouvarda, all over the icons of Mary, especially the silver icon of Panagia Fidoussa, the Virgin of the Snakes.

No one knows where they come from. People touch them and pray, or hold a snake to their head for protection. After 15 August they disappear as mysteriously as they appeared, and they are not seen again for the rest of the year.

The church is at the monastery of Our Lady Of Langouvarda, which was once a nunnery. According to tradition, the nuns were threatened by a pirate attack in 1705. As the invaders approached, the nuns prayed to Mary for help. She heard their prayer and transformed them into snakes. When the pirates entered the convent they saw it full of the creatures and fled, terrified. The reappearance of the snakes is a remembrance of that day. It is said that the only years the snakes don't appear are in times of crisis—the most recent being the German occupation during World War II and the earthquake of 1953, in which the original nunnery was destroyed.

My Mother's Panagia

It seems to me that the most important word in Greek life is **Panagia**—
*the Virgin Mary, all saintly, all holy. Because Mary is human and has
suffered so much, having seen her only child being crucified, she understands the sufferings of others. She is very special for Greeks.*

*Over the centuries, countless miracles and graces have flowed
through Mary's icons. On the island of Tinos, there is an important
church and monastery dedicated to Mary. The church has a miraculous icon to which thousands of people go to pray every year. They pray
for three or four days outside the church, sleeping in sleeping bags.
Pilgrims crawl on their knees down the road from the island's port to
the church, as part of their prayerful offering. Others walk barefoot.
Mary has saved so many people, and the church is full of offerings of
thanksgiving. Usually they are of silver or gold. I owe my life to Mary.
When I was small I was often sick and in hospital. My parents prayed
to her, and when I got well, to thank her they took me and baptised
me in the church on Tinos.*

*My mother Maria comes from a small village called
Kounavi, in Crete. It has two churches, one dedicated to Christ and
one to the Virgin. A tiny chapel is dedicated to Saint George. No
more than five people can fit inside it. On the walls there are old
fresco paintings, but most are flaking off now.*

*In this little chapel there is a mysterious and holy icon of
Mary painted on a piece of cloth. No one really knows the story
behind it, but we do know it is an offering, because written on the
bottom there is a date in the 19th century. Villagers believe this
icon is miraculous, and people in difficult situations often go and
pray before her. She is my mother's special Mary. When I see people
praying, standing in front of the icon, gazing so deeply at Mary, I
am amazed by how they pray and speak to her as if she is standing*

alive in front of them. Some people say that she is gazing back at them. My mother told me that when she prayed she felt that Mary's face became sweeter and full of understanding. Sometimes she even felt that she blinked at her. The Greek love of Mary is something very beautiful and special.

—Ekaterina, *Greece*

The Madonna of Monte Vergine
— Italy —

Monte Vergine has long been considered a holy place. In pre-Christian times, it housed a temple of Cybele, nature goddess and mother of the gods. On the ruins of this ancient temple, a monastery church houses the Byzantine image of Our Lady of Monte Vergine.

In the 12th century, at the age of fifteen, William of Vercelli decided to live in solitude as a hermit on the wild mountain. During this time its name was changed from Monte Virgiliano to Monte Vergine, the Mountain of the Virgin. When William saw an apparition of the Holy Virgin holding the infant Jesus, he realised that Mary wanted a church dedicated to her to be built on the site of the pagan temple. Obeying this holy request, William built a modest chapel. It attracted other hermits, who formed a religious order called Monte Vergine, wearing white habits in honour of Mary's purity.

The tiny building eventually grew into a spectacular basilica, housing an ancient portrait of Mary dating back hundreds of years. The Virgin's deep brown eyes are said to console everyone who gazes into them.

Even today the beautiful mountain path leading up to the basilica is often filled with pilgrims coming to pray before the holy portrait, which has been credited with many miracles. One of them was witnessed by the abbot of the nearby monastery, Don Victor Corvaia. Among a group of pilgrims, the voice of a distraught mother stood out. She had brought her deformed, dying three-year-old son to pray before the image of

Mary. Hearing her heart-rending sobs, other pilgrims were moved to pray for her too, and to offer words of comfort. Crying and wailing, the mother pleaded to the Holy Mother, 'Take him to yourself or else cure him.' To everyone's amazement, the little boy slipped from his mother's arms and ran along the church floor, completely healed. Shouts of joy and gratitude went up from the worshippers: '*Evviva la Madonna!*— Long live the Madonna!'

The Holy Mountain of Mary
— Greece —

All over the globe, there are pockets of land that have an almost mystical beauty. People sense that they are holy places, and many of these places have been consecrated to Mary.

According to one legend, Mary was travelling with Saint John the Evangelist from Joppa to Cyprus to visit Lazarus when their ship was blown off course. Forced to land on the pagan peninsula of Athos, in Greece, the holy woman marvelled at its stark, wild beauty. A high, rocky mountain rose almost sheer from a deep-blue sea. The wonder of it inspired Mary to pray, telling God of her desire to have the mountain as her own. A voice replied, 'Let this place be your inheritance and your garden, a paradise and a haven of salvation for those seeking to be saved.'

Mount Athos is often referred to as Holy Mountain. Located on a 60-km tip of one of the three arms of Halkidiki peninsula, it is the world's oldest monastic republic, where the monks still live according to the Julian calendar. Now a World Heritage site and home to twenty Orthodox monasteries, it is as much Mary's as ever. So much so that no other woman is permitted on the mountain; its population of around 2250 is entirely male. Since an official edict was issued in 1060, women have only ever been allowed on Athos in times of extreme need. The Church of Protaton on Mount Athos houses stunning art works, murals and the Axion Estin, the miraculous holy icon of the Blessed Virgin Mary.

The Serbian monastery of Chiliandari on Mount Athos is also home to the Hodigitria-style icon known as Our Lady With Three Hands. In the eighth century, Saint John Damascene had been debating bitterly with iconoclasts, who claimed that veneration of icons was wrong. Saint John was accused of treason and had his hand amputated as punishment. He took his severed hand and turned to pray before an icon of Mary that, like so many, was attributed to Luke the Evangelist. John fell asleep, and awoke to find his hand miraculously healed. In deep gratitude, he crafted a silver hand and added it to the icon, in the lower left of the picture.

Devoted to lives of prayer and solitude, the monastic communities of Athos seek union with God through the intercession of the Blessed Virgin. The first monks arrived in the third or fourth century, filling the mountainside with the sounds of prayer for over a millennium. It is the only place in Greece, and one of the few places in the world, that is completely devoted to prayer. Covering 350 square kilometres, the 2000-metre-high mountain, adorned with ancient evergreens, has a beauty that transcends time.

O Virgin of the heights in this world, pray for us
O Virgin of ancient miracles, pray for us
Mary, wellspring of peace, be our guide.
—FROM THE PRAYERS FOR MONTSERRAT

The Madonna of Montallegro
— Italy —

O ne warm July in 1557, Giovanni Chichizola was walking home from the markets. The picturesque route took him through Montallegro, a spectacular mountain surrounded by a clear blue gulf stretching out into the Ligurian Sea. Giovanni paused to rest in the shade and heard a gentle voice calling his name. Before him stood the luminescent figure of a beautiful woman in blue and white. She explained that she was Mary and told him to let the local people know of her appearance. As she spoke, Mary gestured to a small wooden painting that was leaning on a rock nearby. 'Tell the people that this picture was brought here from Greece by angels. I leave it here in token of my love for them. Fast on Saturday,' she urged, then vanished.

Amazed, Giovanni gazed at the painting left to his care. It was an image of the Virgin Mary lying in a bier, surrounded by angels, saints and the Holy Trinity. He went eagerly to pick up the painting, but it would not move. So Giovanni called some people nearby to come to his aid. As he told his incredible story, some droplets of water began seeping from the rock where the painting rested.

Leaving the onlookers, Giovanni raced to the nearby town of Rapallo. He convinced a group of sceptical priests to come with him to the picture. They returned to find that the droplets had become a bubbling stream of clear water beside the painting. One of the priests moved the painting quite easily and took it back to the parish church for safe keeping.

The next day, the painting had gone. Giovanni found it on the mountainside again, exactly where it had been the previous day. The local people felt certain that this was where Mary wanted it to be. Tons of rock had to be removed to create a solid foundation for a new church, and the building materials had to be carried almost 700 metres up the mountain. Yet in spite of these challenges, within a year, the church was built and consecrated. In 1574, a group of shipwrecked Greek sailors recognised the miraculous image as a picture that had been venerated in Ragusa until its mysterious disappearance in 1557. After a legal exchange, the sailors took the painting away with

them, only to have it disappear the next day. It reappeared in Montallegro, and never left again.

Many miracles have been attributed to Mary's intercession at Montallegro. Over the years, grateful pilgrims have left so many votive plaques to give thanks for these miracles that whole galleries had to be built to accommodate them. Ancient documents show that Mary's miraculous intervention also saved her people from plagues in 1579, 1590 and again in 1630. Today, the original rock where the painting appeared is still visible in the church, and all these centuries later the miraculous spring continues to flow.

We turn to you for protection
Holy Mother of God.
Listen to our prayers,
and help us in our needs.
Save us from every danger
glorious and blessed Virgin.

—'Sub Tuum Praesidium', oldest known prayer to Mary, found in a Greek papyrus scroll, c. 300 AD

Mary of Montserrat
— Spain —

The mountain range rises more than 1000 metres, forming a harsh and imposing landscape. According to legend, the holy mountain of Montserrat was once a gigantic, smooth boulder. At the moment of Christ's crucifixion, the sky darkened and the rock shook, taking on its present form. It was in this inhospitable terrain that Our Lady of Montserrat was discovered.

One Saturday evening in the ninth century, a group of shepherd boys heard angelic music and saw light radiating from the mountain. Unsure what to do, they told their priest, who in turn called the bishop. When they inspected the mountain more closely they discovered a cave that sheltered a wooden figure of the Blessed Virgin cradling Jesus in one arm and holding an orb in her other other hand. This beautiful Black Madonna turned out to be an ancient carving that had been lost 200 years before.

When the men tried to carry the statue to the cathedral, something strange occurred. Although it was only about a metre tall, they suddenly found they couldn't take it any further. It was too heavy. The bishop surmised that the Virgin Mary wanted to be venerated in the modest chapel of a nearby hermitage. This simple chapel was gradually transformed into a church, and sits about halfway up the mountain, close to where the Madonna was first discovered. It is thought that this precious statue, originally called La Jerosolimitana, the native of Jerusalem, was brought from the Holy Land to Barcelona and hidden in the mountains of Montserrat to avoid Saracen attacks in the eighth century. The isolated sanctuary was once considered a potential hiding place for the holy grail.

La Morenata, the Little Black Madonna, is still venerated today as the patroness of Catalonia, and many turn to her for guidance in marriage. There is a wonderful local phrase that goes, *No es ben casat qui no dun la done a Montserrat*, 'He is not well wed who has not taken his wife to Montserrat.'

The little statue is also said to have inspired Wagner's opera *Parsifal*. One of the mountain's hermits, Bernat Boil, became America's first missionary when he arrived in the New World with Christopher Columbus. One of Monserrat's first abbots became Pope Julius II, who commissioned many of Michaelangelo's works. All of Spain's kings have prayed before La Morenata, as have several saints, including Saint Ignatius of Loyola. After spending the night in prayer before the Little Black Madonna, Ignatius gave up his career as a soldier and went on to become the founder of the Society of Jesus, better known as the Jesuits.

Meeting with Mary

I was born in Spain, in Burgos, in the province of Castille. It is an ancient place, historically important as a rest point for pilgrims on their way to Santiago de Compostela and the tomb of Saint James the Apostle. We have a beautiful cathedral, a medieval castle and high medieval gates. Our patron Madonna is Santa Maria la Mayor, Saint Mary the Great, and our cathedral was named after her.

Mary is there all the time, in the home, in the schools (at least in my time) and in the streets. I especially remember the processions of Holy Week, when the statues were taken out for everyone to see. One procession is called el encuentro—*the encounter or the meeting. It begins on Holy Thursday afternoon and continues until after dark. It is heartbreaking to watch. A statue of Our Lady of Sorrows is taken from one* part of the town to meet Christ bearing the Cross. In two solemn processions through ancient narrow streets, the crowds accompany the Holy Mother and her son. The people walk with heavy, prayerful steps, carrying candles, singing mourning hymns, beating drums.

Everyone has suffering in their lives. I certainly did, and to see Mary crying with seven swords in her heart made me lift up my eyes from my little troubles and realise that there is no pain like her pain. The mother of God, full of grace and full of suffering, humbly walks to meet her son, who suffered so much for love of humanity.

The two wooden statues would meet in front of the cathedral of Santa Maria la Mayor, in the centre of town. The songs and the drums stopped, and the silent darkness lit by the candles was more touching than a thousand words. My complaints and problems seemed as nothing compared with Mary's broken soul as she saw her son with the Cross. The processions did not finish there. Christ continued his procession to Calvary, and Mary did too, both separating for a while until they met again at the foot of the Cross.

I treasure these memories, and they still help me today in my life as a young priest. The intervention of Mary is without doubt what keeps me here, trying, like her, to keep everything in my heart so that I can humbly bring Christ to others.

—Father Jesus, *Western Australia*

. . . *If we are humble, hidden as the Virgin's statue was hidden, we will resurface, as at Montserrat, in glory.*
—CONTEMPLATION ON THE VIRGIN OF MONTSERRAT

Mary of La Salette
— France —

Nestled in the lower slopes of the French Alps is the humble village of La Salette. In the mid-19th century, around 800 people eked a living from the stony land. The French Revolution, the Napoleonic wars, epidemics and near-famine had left them discouraged and apathetic. The future looked bleak.

Melanie Mathieu, fourteen, and Maximin Giraud, eleven, came from very poor families. Melanie had been taught to beg on the streets from a young age. She was illiterate, barely knew her prayers and found occasional work as a farm labourer.

Maximin, by contrast, was hyperactive, high-spirited and mischievous. He was, by his own admission, a frequent liar, and would say whatever it took to get out of trouble. Like Melanie, he had no formal education. He went to church occasionally, but it took him a long time to learn anything, including prayers. He had grown up rough, with a sharp tongue and foul language. At home, life was difficult. His father was an alcoholic and he had a tense relationship with his stepmother.

One day in September 1846, the two children, who hardly knew each other, were put to work tending cattle. It was the eve of the feast of Our Lady of Seven Sorrows, but the children didn't know that, or care. At noon they had lunch and then fell asleep.

Melanie awoke first, and her immediate thought was of the cows. She and Maximin found them grazing contentedly, and the girl went to pack up the leftovers from lunch. Near the edge of a ravine, she caught sight of a bright circle of light shining far below. 'Come quickly!' she called.

Maximin saw it too. Terrified, the two children were about to run when the circle of light began slowly opening. Their eyes made out the form of a woman, sitting on a stone in the ravine with her face in her hands. Her expression was one of deep sorrow. As they stared down at her, they saw she was weeping. Slowly, she stood up. She was the tallest woman they'd ever seen.

As she crossed her arms over her chest, the two children took in her beauty. On her head was a glowing crown. Her robe shone, and a sparkling golden apron fell from her waist to the ground. Her white slippers were adorned with pearls, gold buckles and tiny, multicoloured roses, as was the white shawl that draped over her shoulders. Two golden chains hung about her neck, one wide with large links, the other carrying a golden crucifix with a hammer and pincers on each side.

The children could see through her body to the ground behind her. 'There was nothing in her dress that belonged to earth,' Maximin later wrote. 'It was all of light, but a light quite different from any other.' A second ring of light encircled both the lady and the children. As Maximin and Melanie stared in amazement, they realised that none of their figures cast a shadow.

The beautiful lady spoke in a firm, gentle voice. 'Come to me, my children. Do not be afraid. I am here to tell you something of the greatest importance.' Her perfect French was a little difficult for the children to grasp, as they spoke only the local dialect. Gradually, her words became easier to understand.

Melanie and Maximin went down into the ravine, close enough to the figure to see the tears on her cheeks.

'I have appointed you six days for working,' she said. 'The seventh I have reserved for myself. And no one will give it to me.' She spoke of many concerns that oppressed her heart.

After a while, Melanie realised that she could no longer hear the lady's voice, though her lips were still moving. The lady had turned to Maximin and was confiding a secret for his ears only. Soon she turned to Melanie and spoke. This time, Maximin couldn't hear what she said.

Then she spoke again to both of them. 'If people are converted, the rocks will become piles of wheat,' she said, 'and it will be found that the potatoes have sown themselves.' Then she paused. 'Do you say your prayers well, my children?' she asked.

'No,' they confessed. 'We say them hardly at all.'

'Ah, my children, it is very important to say them, at night and in the morning. When you don't have time, at least say an Our Father and a Hail Mary. And when you can, say more.'

She spoke to the children of her sadness at seeing people absent from church, or going only because they felt they had nothing better to do. And then she asked a rather odd question. 'My children, haven't you ever seen spoiled grain?'

'No, never,' replied Maximin.

'But my child, you must have seen it once, near Coin, with your papa,' she insisted, and proceeded to recount the entire story. 'Your papa gave you a piece of bread and said, "Well, my son, eat some bread this year, anyhow. I don't know who'll be eating any next year, if the grain goes on spoiling like that."'

Maximin suddenly realised she was right. The forgotten incident came back vividly. 'It's very true, Madame,' he said, 'Now I remember it.'

'My children, you will make this known to all my people.' the vision said. Then she turned slowly and began to glide across the ravine. 'You will make this known to all my people,' she repeated.

Melanie and Maximin followed. After a pause, the beautiful lady floated into the air. As she turned her gaze towards heaven, her face glowed with joy and her tears vanished. With a final glance the light around her pulsated, then the vision faded.

'There remained a great light,' Maximin later recalled, 'which I tried to catch with my hands, as well as the flowers she had at her feet; but there was nothing there.'

After a moment's silence, Melanie turned to her companion. 'Perhaps she was a great saint,' she said.

When they brought the cows back in, Maximin told the entire story to his employer. Melanie was still stabling the horses when she was sent for and questioned. Her story matched his account perfectly.

Next morning, the two children were sent to the priest's house at La Salette. 'It must have been the Blessed Virgin whom you saw,' he said. At Mass he related the story to his congregation. Word spread fast about the children's vision.

Afraid that the children were victims of a hoax, the mayor interviewed Melanie. He questioned, cross-examined, threatened, ridiculed, even offered a bribe. Nothing would make her retract or change her story. The meek, impoverished girl seemed beyond corruption, and utterly certain of what she had seen.

By Monday a crowd had begun to gather at the site of the apparition. Where Mary's tears had fallen, an old dried-up spring now flowed with clear water. Many conversions and healings took place at La Salette. Maximin's father was healed of his asthma at the spring and became a devout believer. Sixty thousand pilgrims walked to the apparition site along wild, stony paths—wagons couldn't cross the impenetrable terrain. Twenty-three cures were reported. A church was built from the stones of the surrounding mountain, and a new religious order sprang up, the Missionaries of La Salette—the first order to be named after an apparition of Mary.

Mary's warnings of famine, sickness and poor crops proved prophetic. A potato famine hit Ireland, crops failed everywhere, and cholera epidemics raged throughout Europe.

Did Melanie and Maximin suddenly become pious after seeing Our Lady and inspiring such a spiritual revival? Melanie stayed sullen, Maximin hyperactive. They seemed to retain all the character flaws they had grown up with. Their lack of charm made many doubt their story. But for all their short-comings, Maximin and Melanie refused to profit financially from the apparition and both maintained a love of prayer all their lives.

Years afterwards, the mere mention of the apparition made Melanie and Maximin suddenly solemn. Abbe Dupanloup, who investigated the case, said that the children would 'inspire the listener with a sort of religious awe for their words, and of respect for their persons . . . During the past two years, the two children and their parents have remained as poor as before.'

'Never in a court of justice have culprits been so harassed with questions about the crime with which they were charged, as have been these poor little peasant children, for the past two years, on the matter of this wonderful Event . . . Moreover, the frequent repetition of these trials has never caused them to contradict either themselves, or each other.' These words were from the man whose first impression was of a boy he described as 'repulsive' and a girl who was 'peevish and sulky, and silent because of her stupidity'.

The two simple child visionaries grew into wandering, restless adults. Maximin made a few attempts to study for the priesthood, but his limited early education was a great impediment. He became a medical student, a Papal Guard, a government official in Paris, a merchant. He always had time to relate his story to whoever would listen, and many witnesses testified to the great emotion that would overcome him, as though his whole face was transfigured.

Despite his poverty, he would never accept money from pilgrims. At his lowest point he took flasks of liqueur and herbs labelled with his name and sold them at a chalet near the apparition site. Maximin was desperate and heavily in debt at the time. His partner in the scheme later ran off with all their profits. 'I only did it to earn my living by the sweat of my brow,' he would later say.

Maximin suffered from asthma and heart disease, and died at the age of forty. In his will he affirmed the truth of the apparition one last time. At Maximin's request, his heart was placed in the Basilica of Our Lady on the holy mountain of La Salette.

Melanie tried to join various religious communities, living with the Sisters of Providence in France and with the Carmelites in England. But like Maximin, she could never settle down, and she remained poor. As she grew older she became delusional, imagining many supernatural experiences.

People believed she was a saint for no greater reason than the fact that she had once seen Mary. The tragedy was that she seemed to believe them, enjoying the flattery and adulation. She even published the 'secret' she had received from Mary. Many believed she had written a false account to please the people around her. It was quite a change for the girl who once said, 'I want to tell it only to the Pope. And only when he orders it.'

Still, Melanie prayed often and attended Mass every day. She was preparing for Mass when she died, at the age of seventy-two.

For all society's later demands and pressures, Mary had made only one request of Melanie and Maximin: 'make this known to all my people'. And to that difficult task they successfully devoted the rest of their lives.

Most holy mother, Our Lady of la Salette,
Who for love of me shed such bitter tears
In your merciful apparition,
Look down with kindness upon me.
—PRAYER OF THE LA SALETTE MISSIONARIES

Mary's Perpetual Help
— Italy —

O ne of the most enduring images of Mary is the painting of Our Lady of Perpetual Help, or Our Lady of Perpetual Succour. It blends the symbolism of eastern icons with the tenderness of western art to create what some have called the perfection of all icons.

Its long and mysterious history extends back to 13th century Crete, where an unknown monk painted Our Lady of Perpetual Help inspired by the Old Testament prophecy of Isaiah: 'My sufferings are always before me.' Mary wears red, the colour of an Eastern empress's robes and the colour worn by virgins in Christ's time. Her dark-blue mantle is of a colour worn by mothers in Palestine. She holds the infant Jesus, a full grown person in miniature, symbolising his divinity.

This image was brought to Rome by a merchant in 1499. Some say he stole the image from a church in Crete. Others suggest he was a pious man whose dying wish was to have the image displayed in a church for public veneration. Perhaps both stories are true.

No one knew where to keep the icon, until the merchant's daughter encountered a beautiful lady who gave her a message. 'Tell your mother that Holy Mary of Perpetual Succour wishes her icon to be venerated in the church that stands between the Basilica of St Mary Major and the Basilica of St John Lateran.'

As the lady requested, the icon was placed in the Church of San Matteo. For nearly 300 years, pilgrims came to pray before the icon, which became known as the Madonna di San Matteo. Many miracles were attributed to it.

One exhausted little boy was dragged along on pilgrimage by his parents, from the Basilica of St Mary Major to the Basilica of St John Lateran. To his great relief they let him rest in the Church of San Matteo. There, his little eyes gazed upon Our Lady of Perpetual Help, and he fell in love. It was an image his heart would never forget, and he would one day play an important role in the icon's story.

In the 17th century, the Church of San Matteo became a haven for persecuted Irish priests until it was burned during the French invasion of Italy. One survivor, Augustinian Brother Augustine Orsetti, escaped with a cart of old furniture. Among his possessions was Our Lady of Perpetual Help, safely hidden beneath a torn cloak. The exhausted brother found shelter in the Church of St Eusebius, where he stayed with his precious icon for twenty-one years. He then moved to a monastery in Posterula, bringing his beloved icon with him. Brother Augustine waited patiently for thirty-four years, praying for the time when great crowds would venerate her once again. It was a day he would not live to see. But he would not let her beauty die with him.

A schoolboy, Michael Marchi, used to come to the monastery each morning to help the brothers and serve at Mass. 'Michael! Michael!' the elderly Brother Augustine would call. He would point adoringly at the beautiful image. '*That* is the original icon of Our Lady of Perpetual Help.' His eyes would soften as his heart filled with memories. 'Everyone now has forgotten. Do not *you* forget. Remember, Michael, it is miraculous.'

Two years later, Michael found himself in Rome, watching work on a new Redemptorist monastery under construction on the site of the old Church of San Matteo. Eventually, he himself joined the order.

One evening, a casual conversation with another priest led to speculation about the fate of the miraculous icon that had disappeared from San Matteo so many years before. 'Possibly it was destroyed with the church,' one priest suggested. But Father Michael Marchi knew better, and the words of his elderly friend rang in his ears: 'Everyone now has forgotten. Do not you forget.'

'I have prayed often before that icon,' he said. 'It may still be in Saint Mary's Posterula.'

The young priest tracked down the old painting in the place where he had grown up with it. 'It was abandoned,' he was to recall. 'Not so much as a candle burned before it. I had often served Mass there and looked up wonderingly at it.'

In 1865, the Redemptorists met with Pope Pius IX to tell him the whole extraordinary story. Listening intently, the Pope thought back to his youth, and a moment of relief during a long, exhausting trip with his parents. A young boy, sitting in awe before a beautiful image he had never forgotten.

After a moment of silence, he spoke. 'I remember the icon well,' he said. 'Years ago, when I was a child, my parents made a pilgrimage from St Mary Major to St John Lateran. I grew tired on the way. They brought me to the Church of San Matteo to rest. There I saw the icon, and immediately I loved it.'

He seemed to know exactly what to do. Taking a pen, he wrote, 'It is our will that the image of Most Holy Mother Mary be returned to its place between the two Basilicas of St John and St Mary Major.'

So Our Lady of Perpetual Help found her new home in the new Church of St Alphonsus, on the same road, Via Merulana, as its old location in Rome.

By now the icon was beginning to show its age. But although it was faded and worm-eaten, with nails clumsily driven into it, its grace and beauty still shone through. The Polish iconographer Leopold Novodny restored the image, praying as he painted and painting as he prayed. In a grand public procession through the streets of Rome and before crowds of thousands, the lovingly restored icon was taken to its new home in the Church of St Alphonsus.

While the street celebrations were going on, in a nearby home a mother was comforting her dying child. In desperation she held her child through the open window. 'Mary, cure my child,' she cried, 'or take him to heaven!'

Only three days later, the little boy was lighting a candle in the Church of St Alphonsus, praying before Our Lady of Perpetual Help in thanksgiving for a miracle. Like the young Pope Pius IX and Michael Marchi before him, the child fell in love with Our Lady of Perpetual Help. The window of his home was never closed again. Instead, a copy of the icon sits on the sill, gazing down into Via Merulana.

For three days the icon was enshrined above the altar, and 50,000 people prayed before it. Pope Pius IX was among the first to visit it in its new home. He prayed with as much tender devotion as he had so many years before, when he had fallen in love with Our Lady as a young boy in the Church of San Matteo. Along with possession of the icon and responsibility for it, the Pope gave the Redemptorists just one command: 'Make her known.'

Since then, 2300 copies of the icon have been sent from the Church of St Alphonsus in Rome to churches, shrines and homes all over the world.

My name is Mother of Perpetual Help
No century or country can claim me.
I belong to all ages and all peoples.
Many names have been given to me. I have been called
the 'Virgin of the Passion', 'the Golden Madonna',
'the Mother of the Redemptorist Missionaries',
'the Mother of Catholic homes'.
The name of my own choosing is 'Mother of Perpetual Help'.
    —W.D. CREEDE, REDEMPTORIST PRAYER

Mary of the Desert
— Kuwait —

In January 1864, a Carmelite missionary from Baghdad, Father Mary-Joseph of Jesus, decided to go to Europe to fetch more priests to assist in his work. During his journey through the desert, he passed near the ruins of Birs-Nemrod, in today's Iraq, said to be the ruins of the Tower of Babel. Knowing that he had a long and perilous journey ahead, he decided to consecrate the ruins to the Blessed Virgin Mary as a prayer for safe passage. Climbing on to the ancient, crumbling walls, he placed a glittering medal in a crevice and, proclaiming Mary Queen of the Desert, promised to erect a statue of Mary in place of the medal if he arrived home safely.

As he made his way to Damascus, bedouins twice attacked his caravan, but each time he escaped unharmed. When he reached Paris, he preached at the Basilica of Our Lady of Victories, talking of his trip through the desert and of his promise to return. Inspired by his words, a group of women collected enough money to buy a bronze statuette of Our Lady of Victories. Father Joseph-Mary took it with him to Lyons and Rome and back to Baghdad. With a group of the faithful he returned to the ruins of Birs-Nemrod. Celebrating Mass, he placed the little statue among the fallen stones, fulfilling his promise to Mary of the Desert.

The Lady of the Stars
— France —

The people of Pontmain in northwestern France were largely peasant farmers, hard workers who lived off the land. Apart from the normal difficulties of such a life, in early 1871 they were faced with the threat of invasion. Paris was under siege. The Prussians had conquered Strasbourg, Metz, Orléans, and Le Mans, and stopped only a few kilometres short of Laval. Surely Pontmain, just fifty kilometres further on, would be the next target? In desperation the people of Pontmain turned to prayer.

Early one January evening, Joseph and Eugène Barbedette were doing their usual after-school chores, pounding horseshoes, crushing gorse, grinding feed for the animals in the barn that doubled as their bedroom. It was half past five and freezing cold. A neighbour came to chat with their father, César, and Eugène took the opportunity to take a break and look up into the dark sky. 'I went to see what the weather was like,' he recalled later.

The morning's snow still clung to the land like a soft, white blanket. The deep-blue sky was clear and sprinkled with bright stars. Only a strange patch of dark blue, above a neighbour's house, had no stars in it.

Eugène looked curiously at the dark patch. Where were the stars he was so familiar with? As he stared into the night, something brighter than any star emerged to meet his gaze. It was a beautiful woman, standing in the sky. Her deep-blue gown seemed embroidered with golden stars. Beltless, it draped elegantly down to her blue slippers, each adorned with a golden rosette. A golden crown rested on her head, atop a black veil that fell gently down her back.

She smiled, and Eugène was enchanted. He gazed upon her for about fifteen minutes before Jeanette, their neighbour, interrupted his reverie. Eugène pointed to the lady and asked Jeanette if she saw anything. She saw only sky. When his father came, he had to agree with her. But young Joseph saw the same woman quite easily.

César was annoyed at what was obviously a childish prank and sent the boys back into the barn, asking Jeanette to tell no one of his sons' foolishness. After she left, César asked Eugène to check and see if the figure was still there. Sure enough, she was.

He sent the boy to fetch his mother, Victoire, but she too could see nothing in the sky. Still, taken aback by her sons' insistence, she suggested that they pray five Our Fathers and five Hail Marys.

Curious neighbours began to emerge, but the family avoided any explanation and retreated to the barn. Victoire fetched her spectacles and still couldn't see the lady in the sky. Their servant also saw nothing. The boys were told off and the adults, feeling foolish, urged them into the house for dinner. Joseph managed to obtain permission for him and Eugène to return to the barn afterwards, on condition that they again recite five Our Fathers and five Hail Marys. So they gulped down their meal and soon rushed off. 'She's still there, and as tall as Sister Vitaline!' cried the boys.

The sister, a nun who taught in Pontmain's small school, was fetched to see if perhaps she could see the strange vision. All she saw was a strange triangle of three stars. 'The lady's head is in the middle of them,' explained Eugène.

Soon even the boys' sceptical parents could perceive the three stars. Perhaps, then, only children could see the vision?

The three boarding students were fetched from the Pontmain school, eleven-year-old Françoise Richer, nine-year-old Jeanne-Marie Lebossé, and thirteen-year-old Augustine Mouton.

Françoise was the first of the girls to see Our Lady. As she reached the local cobbler's house, she cried out, 'I can see something on the Guidecoqs' house but I don't know what it is.' Continuing on a few steps towards the barn, she cried out together with Jeanne-Marie, 'Oh! The beautiful lady!'

Nuns and housekeepers came, and grandmothers carrying their grandchildren. Soon half the village was gathered at the barn, all bringing their children in the hope that they could see Our Lady. All the witnesses could see the triangle of stars that surrounded Mary's face. But only a few saw the beautiful lady herself.

Among them was a sickly child, six-year-old Eugène Friteau. He was carried there, wrapped in his grandmother's mantle, but could only stay outside the barn for a little while because of the chill. He passed away in May that year, but before he died, he said he too had seen Mary that night, just as the others had described her.

Another possible witness was two-year-old Augustine, who came with her mother, Madame Boitin, the cobbler's wife. The little girl waved and clapped towards the apparition, and called excitedly, 'Le Jésus! Le Jésus!' It was the only religious word she knew.

The crowd had now grown to about sixty people, including the parish priest, Father Guérin. Though they saw nothing but three strange stars, it was clear that something extraordinary was happening. All at once, the children cried out loud—something was changing. An oval-shaped frame was forming around the lady, in a blue the same deep blue as her gown. Four candles, two at the level of the shoulders and two at the knees, appeared around her, and a small red cross materialised over her heart.

Some people grew distracted and began to chatter and make irreverent jokes. One man insisted that with a telescope he would be able to see the lady, but when one was fetched it proved ineffective. The crowd laughed. Then the children told them that the lady had stopped smiling and was looking down upon them with great sadness.

Father Guérin insisted they maintain a silent reverence before the vision, and suggested that they pray the rosary. 'If the children only are privileged to behold the celestial vision,' he surmised, 'it is because they are more worthy than we.'

The adults knelt on the snowy ground and began to pray while the children stood and gazed at Mary. As the rosary continued, the figure and its frame grew until it seemed twice the size of a normal human figure, and Mary beamed with the most radiant smile. The stars seemed to move aside for her. From faraway and nearby, stars began to multiply and drifted onto her dress and her feet, sparkling like diamonds.

The chilly winter air began to take its toll on the people in the group, who saw none of this spectacular display. They crowded into the barn for warmth, still peering into the sky through the open doors. The four visionary children remained standing in the doorway. As the rosary concluded they began another prayer, the Magnificat. 'Something new is happening!' cried the children.

A white banner had appeared in the sky and unfurled itself at the foot of the Virgin. About a metre wide, it seemed to stretch out along the length of the neighbour's house.

A golden line appeared, and then revealed itself as a letter.

'It's an M!' cried the children, 'and now there is another letter—it's an A!'

Soon an entire word was formed, *mais*—but. It remained in the sky for about ten minutes. Suddenly another local man burst on the scene, announcing that the Prussians were now at Laval, just on their doorstep! To his astonishment, the crowd seemed unperturbed. 'They could have been at the entrance of the village and we would not be afraid,' said one woman.

The prayers continued, and more letters appeared. Soon a phrase was formed: *But pray, my children*. Many were moved to tears. More letters: *God will hear you in a short time*. Mary smiled and laughed sweetly at their astonishment.

They began to sing the Inviolata as a second line of words appeared beneath the first. *My son . . .*

The children were elated. 'It is really the Blessed Virgin!' they cried . . . *permits himself to be moved*.

A large golden line appeared under the sentence, as if to emphasise it.

Tears and prayers flowed from the crowd. The lady in the sky was moved to a different emotion. 'Look, she's laughing!' exclaimed the visionaries, jumping and clapping with joy. 'Oh, how beautiful she is! How beautiful!'

The joy of the children infected the crowd, and now everyone was laughing and crying and praying. It was a strange and beautiful scene: a celestial mother laughing with her children.

Recollecting themselves, the people began to sing a hymn that had been composed in Pontmain: 'Mother of hope, of name so sweet, protect our country, pray for us, pray for us.'

Mary raised her arms as they sang the eight verses. Her hands and fingers seemed to move in time to the music, as if she was conducting or playing an invisible instrument.

As the song concluded, the words at her feet faded away, and after another hymn, her face grew sad. It seemed as though she tried to speak, but no words were heard. A red crucifix appeared before Mary. The figure of Christ on it was an even deeper red. Taking the cross in her hands, Mary held it towards the children as a white banner unfurled at its top. In red letters the name 'Jesus Christ' appeared before them.

The people sang, and Mary prayed with them. For as long as he lived, Joseph would never forget the sadness on

Mary's face as she beheld the cross. A star emerged and lit the four candles that surrounded Mary, then came to rest above her head.

The crowd continued to sing as the crucifix disappeared. Mary, with arms extended, now took the position of Our Lady as she appears on the miraculous medal. Above each of her shoulders, two small white crosses formed.

As the people moved on to reciting the evening prayers and began the examination of conscience, a period of silent contemplation, the children observed a white veil at the lady's feet, which rose up and gradually obscured their view of her. Eventually only the tip of her crown remained. It hung in the sky, surrounded by stars, the four candles and the blue circle that had enshrined the lady. After a moment, they were all gone.

'Do you still see anything?' asked Father Guérin.

'No Monsieur le Curé,' replied the boys. 'It's all over.'

After over three hours of prayers, the apparition had ended, at around 9 p.m. The crowd returned to their homes filled with peace.

Eleven days later, an armistice was signed with Prussia. The war was over. For some reason the Prussian forces never took Laval, and despite their previous military success they never advanced any further after the night of the apparition. All thirty-eight soldiers from Pontmain returned home unharmed.

As for the meaning of the words *But pray my children, God will hear you in a short time. My son permits himself to be moved*, it has been surmised that Our Lady was consoling the people of Pontmain, advising that their prayers for peace would surely be heard. Her son—Jesus—is open, to hear and respond lovingly to the cries of his people. Pope Léon XIII gave the Pontmain apparition the title Our Lady of Prayer. She seemed to appear at a time when prayer was needed, and in response to prayer, to encourage her people to cry out to God.

The fruits of such prayer were seen vividly in the lives of the visionaries. Joseph and Eugène Barbedette both became priests. They were very humble and only ever spoke of the apparition out of duty or obedience.

Françoise lived a simple, devout life, becoming a housekeeper to Father Eugène Barbedette. She died in 1915, with both Barbedette brothers at her side. Jeanne-Marie Lebossé joined the sisters of the Holy Family of Bordeaux, taking the name of Sister Saint-André. She too was remembered for her great humility, compassion, kindness, and great skill as an artist. After being paralysed for ten years, she passed away in 1933.

Pilgrims soon flocked to the site where Our Lady had appeared. On the first anniversary of the apparition, 8000 travelled to Pontmain, mostly by foot or cart. In September 1873, 40,000 pilgrims were recorded. After Mass in the small parish church, they would go to pray at the barn.

A large basilica was built at Pontmain. Devotion to Mary continues to spread worldwide. At the National Shrine of the Immaculate Conception in Washington, DC, there is a chapel dedicated to Our Lady of Hope of Pontmain, built with the help of the comedian Bob Hope and his wife Dolores.

Thousands still come to Pontmain every year, inspired by love for the beautiful woman in the sky who led her children in prayer over 135 years ago.

Mary teaches us how to pray . . . Mary never tires of asking the children to pray.
—POPE PAUL VI, 30 MAY 1971,
THE CENTENARY OF THE APPARITION AT PONTMAIN

Mary of Knock
— Ireland —

The village of Knock, in the west of Ireland, sits in flat, barren, desolate country. In 1879, Knock was little more than a small group of thatched cottages amid poor fields.

Legend held that Saint Patrick had travelled through Knock and blessed it, predicting that one day it would become a great centre of pilgrimage and devotion. That promise seemed no more than an ancient and foolish dream now. But despite poverty and frequent famine, the community was a faithful and prayerful one. The sturdy little church was the centre of the community. The priest, Archdeacon Cavanagh, had a great love for the poor and a deep devotion to Mary, whom he loved to call the ever Immaculate Mother of God. The year before, a great storm had badly damaged the church, and its statues were crushed. The archdeacon ordered two new statues from Dublin, but both were broken in transit. Undeterred, he ordered more statues, and this time they safely arrived, including a statue of Our Lady of Lourdes.

One August evening, Mary McLoughlin, the archdeacon's housekeeper, set off to visit some friends, a respectable family by the name of Beirne. They had been doing comparatively well and had just returned from a short holiday. The weather was atrocious—cold and raining heavily—but the housekeeper went out anyway.

Passing the gable of the church sacristy, she glanced at some figures that seemed to be leaning against the wall. More of the archdeacon's statues, no doubt, but it was a very strange scene. She later said, she 'thought the whole thing very strange'. It seemed a bit foolish to leave them out in the rain like that.

Other passers-by also noticed unusual figures at the church. One woman also assumed they were statues. 'Another collection, God help us!' she thought. A sixteen-year-old girl saw 'something luminous', but it never occurred to her to investigate further. The wild weather pushed all the travellers on, and no one stopped to look.

Mary McLoughlin finally arrived at the home of her friend Mrs Beirne and her daughter Mary, a quiet, intelligent girl who was well liked by everyone. After a short stay, Mary walked Mary McLoughlin home, and this time it was young Mary's turn to notice the strange sight at the church. 'Look at the beautiful figures!' she exclaimed. 'When did the archdeacon put those statues at the gable?'

As Mary McLoughlin gazed towards the church, she realised with a shock that Archdeacon Cavanagh hadn't put any statues there. No rain or wind or sleet could hold back the two excited women as they hurried on towards the church. It suddenly became clear that what they saw was no ordinary collection of statues. These figures moved. The two women stopped in amazement, at 'such a sight as you never saw in your life'.

Mary Beirne ran to fetch her relatives. Then, as the story spread across the small community, more people gathered to see the glowing apparition at the church gable.

One of them was Patrick Hill, an ordinary eleven-year-old who later related what had happened: 'On that day I was drawing home turf, or peat from the bog, on an ass. While at my aunt's at eight o'clock in the evening, Dominic Byrne came into the house; he cried out: "Come up to the chapel and see the miraculous lights, and the beautiful visions that are to be seen there." I followed him . . .'

At the church, 'we immediately beheld the lights; a clear white light covering most of the gable, from the ground up to the window and higher. It was a kind of changing bright light, going sometimes up high and again not so high. We saw figures—the Blessed Virgin, Saint Joseph and Saint John and an altar with a lamb on the altar, and a cross behind the lamb. I went up closer; I saw everything distinctly.'

No words passed between the figures and their entranced audience, or between the figures in that holy scene. At certain moments the light was so dazzling the figures shone like silver. One woman went closer to embrace Mary and found only the hardness of the cold wall behind her. She said she seemed to recede as she reached out, though she smiled at her.

Patrick's was not the only account. Fifteen people aged five to seventy-five saw the unusual display, which lasted for around two hours. From the fifteen witnesses came fifteen varied descriptions of the sight. But they were united on some common points. Bathed in an unearthly, beautiful glow, three life-sized figures floated about two feet in the air by the church gable. Mary, clothed in a white robe, wore a kind of crown. Her hand and eyes were raised upwards in prayer. To her right, Saint Joseph had his head turned as if gazing lovingly upon her. A third figure, Saint John, stood on Mary's other side. Dressed in bishop-like robes with a small mitre, he held an open book in one hand and had the other hand raised as if preaching. Patrick Hill came close enough to make out the letters on the book's pages.

To Saint John's left, a little lamb was standing on a plain altar facing Mary. The rain pelted down all around this strange scene, yet all within it remained completely dry. Not a drop of water seemed to fall in the direction of the gable.

The group prayed the rosary together in the pouring rain. When it all ended, the drenched witnesses tentatively touched the earth around the gable, where the apparition had appeared. Here the gable, and ground, were completely dry.

All the witnesses instinctively felt that the woman must be the Virgin Mary. It seemed natural enough, then, that the greying, bearded man would be Saint Joseph. Mary Beirne was the first to identify the third figure as Saint John the Evangelist, the beloved disciple of Jesus. There was a 'coincidence of figure and pose', she said, between this figure and a statue of Saint John that she had once seen. 'But I am not in any way sure what saint or character the figure represented,' she later admitted. 'I said that it was Saint John the Evangelist, and then all the others present said the same.'

Some saw a cross on the altar behind the lamb. Patrick saw angels around it. Others saw small golden lights like stars, or a halo, around the lamb. Some saw movement in the figures; others saw only a still scene, like a strange tableau from heaven, frozen in time.

Remarkably, the apparition seemed to reach out beyond the scope of a few fortunate visionaries. One man living on the outskirts of the village observed a brilliant light in the distance, in the direction of the church. He was about half a mile from the scene at the time. 'It appeared to me to be a very large globe of golden light,' he later recalled.

Mary McLoughlin went to tell Archdeacon Cavanagh about the amazing display, but he thought she said it was all over. It is also possible that he doubted his housekeeper, who had gone through a phase of excessive drinking. Whatever the reason, he never went out, which, he later admitted, 'I have regretted ever since.' But he bore his loss philosophically. 'God may will that the testimony to his Blessed Mother's presence should come from the simple faithful and not through his priests.'

The Irish clergy asked the media to keep the matter quiet while it was under investigation. The witnesses were interrogated and found to be credible and solid. Experiments with lights and magic lanterns failed to recreate the apparition.

But news still spread by word of mouth. Crowds swarmed to the modest church. Ten days after the apparition, a deaf child was healed. Many other illnesses were miraculously cured at Knock, from blindness and epilepsy to cancer and tuberculosis. People scraped at the cement on the gable until Archdeacon Cavanagh was forced to have its foundations reinforced. As pieces of cement were sent around the world, reports of cures came back. A nun in an Arabian convent wrote in thanks for a piece of cement that she'd used to heal another nun of a wasting disease.

Knock also inspired people to revive traditional Gaelic forms of prayer. Pilgrims kept an all-night prayer vigil on the eve of great feast days. They did rounds of the church grounds, reciting rosaries and litanies aloud. This slow, meditative walking prayer was known as doing or making a station. Sometimes stations were made on bare knees, in the manner of early Irish Christians. Many cures were reported by pilgrims as they made stations.

For the deaf, Knock has a special significance. In 2006, in Mary's month of May, an international pilgrimage to the shrine of Our Lady of Knock was organised for around 200 deaf people.

'For deaf people the non-verbal message of Knock is a very special sign,' said Deacon Karl Josef Arnold, one of the organisers of the pilgrimage. 'They cannot hear, so they would not be able to understand a spoken message. For them, the hearing, and the seeing of the heart is so important—they need signs.' Among the devoted followers of Our Lady of Knock was Pope John Paul II, who made a personal pilgrimage to the church in 1979 to mark the 100th anniversary of the apparition. Mother Teresa of Calcutta also visited some years later.

Once, the desolate, lonely village was called Cnoc, derived from the Gaelic word for hill. Today, it is Cnoc

Mhuire—Mary's Hill. A million or more pilgrims are still estimated to visit Knock each year, and over 300 miraculous cures have been reported. Saint Patrick's prophecy has been fulfilled.

Bright angels are listening with rapture,
To murmurs of welcome so sweet,
From the grief-laden hearts of poor Erin,
Their own Mother Mary to greet!
From heath-covered hilltop and valley,
From every green leaf on the sod,
A ce'ad mi'le fa'ilte is rising
To welcome the Mother of God!

—ANONYMOUS POEM PUBLISHED IN *THE CORK EXAMINER*, 1880

The Black Madonna of Czestochowa
— Poland —

On the limestone hills between Krakow and Wielun in Poland, on the banks of the River Warta, the medieval city of Czestochowa protects an ancient Marian treasure. Our Lady of Czestochowa has survived centuries of war and the ravages of time. She has travelled from Jerusalem under Roman rule to the forests of eastern Europe. She has survived Nazi occupation and a communist regime, and become the twice-crowned Queen of Poland. A great protectress, intercessor and healer, she is still greatly beloved by her many loyal subjects.

According to legend, the icon of Our Lady of Czestochowa began life as a simple wooden table made by Jesus when he was working as an apprentice carpenter under his foster father, Joseph. The evangelist Luke is said to have painted this Black Madonna while listening to Mary talk about her son. Legend has it that on its way to Poland it passed through Constantinople and Russia, and was revered by kings and saints, including the Emperor Charlemagne and Saint Helena, mother of Constantine the Great.

One of the many stories of Our Lady of Czestochowa began in the 14th century, in the deep forests of Belsz, in what is today eastern Poland. The Polish prince, Ladislaus Opolszyk, came across the holy icon in a castle at Belz, where it had been revered for 500 years. It was a time of war, with the countryside overrun by Tartars. One day, a Tartar arrow flew into a window of the castle chapel and pierced the Madonna's throat.

It was the first of her many permanent scars. To keep the icon safe, Prince Ladislaus decided to take it to his home town of Opala. Making a stop at Czestochowa, he left the painting overnight in a small wooden chapel on a hill. The next day he placed it carefully in his carriage and prepared to move on, but the horses refused to budge. No matter what he and his aides did, the horses stood firm. Clearly, the Virgin had chosen her home and would not be moved. Ladislaus took the hint and reverently returned the image to the little chapel, the Church of the Assumption. The day of this miracle, 26 August, is now the painting's feast day. Over the next few years, the church and monastery of Jasna Góra—Bright Hill—were built to house the shrine of the Black Madonna, and it has remained in Czestochowa ever since.

As the image's miraculous reputation spread, pilgrims came from everywhere with valuable offerings for Our Lady. On Easter Day, 1430, a gang of thieves broke into the chapel, looted the monastery and tried to escape in a wagon. But, like Prince Ladislaus, they found that their horses refused to move from Jasna Góra. Furious, the robbers flung the image to the ground, breaking it into three pieces, then slashed it with swords and trampled it in the mud.

Restorers gathered the pieces and struggled to repaint the icon. Some say the image was erased and a completely new Black Madonna was painted on the original panel. Another story claims that the thieves failed to destroy the precious painting and merely scarred it.

The attack served only to strengthen devotion to Our Lady of Czestochowa. Pilgrims came in even greater numbers, and the village became a bustling city. A larger church had to be built to accommodate the crowds.

In 1655 Czestochowa came under siege from the Swedish army. Poland's three major cities—Warsaw, Krakow and Poznan—had already fallen. And when the 3000-strong

Swedish force reached the gates of Jasna Góra, they were met by fewer than 200 soldiers, a handful of noblemen and seventy monks. Their situation seemed hopeless, but the love of Mary inspired them.

The battle lasted for forty days, and the defenders won. Their victory was attributed to Our Lady of Czestochowa, who not only gave comfort to her followers but inspired the entire country to rise up and repel the Swedes. In humble thanksgiving, the Polish king vowed to consecrate his realm to the Mother of God, and proclaimed her its patron and queen. Ever since, Jasna Góra has been a centre of devotion to Mary, to freedom and to national pride. The holy shrine also became a fortress, and continued to repel attacks over the centuries.

The 18th century brought new challenges. The country was divided up and ruled by three foreign powers—Austria, Prussia and Russia. During these difficult years of occupation, the shrine at Jasna Góra remained a silent witness to Polish strength and the loving protection of Mary. Poland's foreign rulers banned pilgrimages, but nothing could banish the Black Madonna's powerful presence in the hearts of the Polish people.

In 1920, the invading Russian Bolshevik army reached the River Vistula, at the threshold of the city of Warsaw. The battle raged during the feast of the Assumption, the day celebrating Mary's rise into heaven. Thousands of pilgrims came to Jasna Góra to pray for a miracle. Just when defeat seemed imminent, the Virgin Mary appeared in the clouds over Warsaw, and the Russian forces suddenly withdrew. The event became known as the miracle of the Vistula.

During the Great Depression, when many people suffered in extreme poverty, Our Lady of Czestochowa continued to encourage and inspire them. In 1932, an astonishing 750,000 pilgrims defied joblessness and economic gloom to celebrate the 550th anniversary of the holy image's arrival in Jasna Góra.

Dedication to Mary does not spare people from trials, but gives them strength for what lies ahead. Later that decade Poland faced one of its greatest tests as Nazi troops invaded Jasna Góra. Political oppression, religious persecution and concentration camps threatened to crush the nation. Despite a strict ban on pilgrimages, half a million Poles visited Jasna Góra in secret during the occupation. At the end of the war, a further one and a half million made the journey there in prayerful gratitude for their liberation.

But Nazi occupation was succeeded by communist domination, and the religious oppression continued. In spite of the danger, devotion to Mary continued to thrive underground. In 1957 a replica of Our Lady of Czestochowa blessed by Pope Pius XII travelled throughout Poland, to the delight of oppressed Poles. When the Soviet Union collapsed and the communists were driven from government, people hailed their liberation as the new miracle of the Vistula. Our Lady of Czestochowa had answered her people's prayers.

For many Poles the high points of Jasna Góra's recent history were the visits of the first Polish Pope, John Paul II. He too had lived through the trials of Nazi persecution and communist oppression, and he had a special love for Our Lady of Czestochowa. Known for his tremendous devotion to Mary, he echoed the prayers of his people for over a thousand years. 'Mary's will is being fulfilled,' he said. 'Here I am . . . I have come . . . The servant called from this land, summoned from the foot of Jasna Góra where I used to stop like you do and where I used to kneel on the bare ground like you often do for hours and hours . . . Mother, I am yours and all that I have is yours.' And he set his offering on the altar before Mary: a single golden rose.

The face of Our Lady of Czestochowa has changed over the centuries, scarred by violent aggressors and darkened by the ravages of time and smoke. It is impossible to tell how much of the painting appears now as it was originally intended. An examination in 1952 revealed that it was painted on lime wood rather than cypress, as the legend claimed, and that its 15th-century restorers had treated the painting in Byzantine style.

Tradition holds that when the Virgin arrived at Jasna Góra, the image was adorned with precious items, which were nailed in place. After its restoration in 1430, the backdrop was permanently adorned with sheets of silver and gold. In some ceremonies, the icon is lovingly robed in priceless antique garments. Of the nine robes that survive, several contain coral, diamonds, rubies and rare gems dating back as far as the 15th century. Each robe has a name. One, called the Robe of Fidelity, is encrusted with rubies and wedding rings for the Holy Virgin, bride of the nation. For devotees, Mary's robes only enhance the icon's beauty.

It is estimated that in the last few years over four million pilgrims have travelled to Jasna Góra, many on foot, to visit the silent, faithful guide and guardian of an entire nation.

Our Lady of Czestochowa, victorious Queen of Poland! We stand before you, O Mother. For six centuries you have been gazing down from your miraculous picture on Jasna Góra into the depths of our hearts and our spirits . . .

—From a prayer of gratitude to Our Lady of Czestochowa

MARY, BLACK AND BEAUTIFUL

Many miracles and dramatic histories have been attributed to Our Lady of Czestochowa, but apart from her powerful intercession she is also famous for her looks. For she is one of hundreds of statues and icons known as Black Madonnas or Black Virgins. Some are dark-skinned by design; others have developed their unusual colouring.

The great monastic writer Saint Bernard of Clairvaux was fervently devoted to Mary. He saw Mary as the bride of God and believed this was reflected in the Song of Songs, the great Old Testament poem about the love between a man and his bride. The woman in the poem declares, 'I am black but beautiful' (*negra sum sed formosa*), and it is believed that artists may have painted Black Madonnas to illustrate this line. Legend records a very personal encounter between Saint Bernard and the Black Virgin of Affligem, in Belgium. Saint Bernard was struggling with writer's block at the time. When he greeted the Madonna with a reverent 'Ave, Maria', she replied with the more informal, 'Salve, Bernarde', and told him to 'get on with his writing'.

Some writers have suggested that Black Madonnas are remnants of pre-Christian goddess worship. Ancient images were adapted to represent Mary, making the transition to Christianity easier. Where the blackness seems to cover the whole painting, of course, it's likely to be the toll taken by centuries of smoke from candles and incense. Many modern Black Madonnas are deliberately made dark-skinned as an artistic choice in African churches. For other ancient Black Madonnas, the meaning behind their dark skin remains a mystery.

'I am black, but beautiful . . .'
—Song of Songs 1:5

A Life with Our Lady of Czestochowa

I grew up in a big city 200 kilometres from Jasna Góra. We used to travel up to see our grandmother, and on every trip we would also stop to see Our Holy Mother—Our Lady of Czestochowa.

I have always loved her. But I didn't always know her so well. I grew up in communist Poland, where religion wasn't taught in schools. We had after-school catechism classes, though, where I was taught to pray to Mary. She was a girl like me, so she'd understand me and my problems better! At least that's what I thought at first. In praying to Mary I came to know and love her son.

In 1983, I was a young student. Pope John Paul II had just announced that this would be a Holy Year, marking 1950 years since Christ died and rose again. It was early August, and Poland was at the peak of the Czestochowa pilgrimage season. My friends and I were sitting around one day over coffee, just chatting. One asked, 'What shall we do to celebrate this special Holy Year?' The answer was obvious. 'Let's go to see our mother, Our Lady of Czestochowa!'

So we arranged to join a pilgrimage group leaving Warsaw. It was 220 kilometres to Czestochowa, and we walked it. It wasn't just a small group of uni student friends. We ended up in a group of 3000 people. And ours was just one of about twelve groups of 100 to 400 people. Many people loved Mary and were willing to walk for her.

Every day, rising at 6 a.m., we walked with backpacks, and every night we slept in tents. We'd have Mass, pray the rosary, sing hymns and listen to talks. We'd stop for short rests, and it seemed that every place we stopped at had a little shrine to Our Lady, from the many pilgrims who had come before us over many centuries.

In rain or shine we walked. It didn't take long to become exhausted. But we were so excited, we hardly slept. We'd walk and sing and pray and share stories of faith. It was wonderful. At the end of a long day we'd stop for dinner and freshen up, then at 9 p.m. everyone would gather again for the hymn to Our Lady.

Everyone walked to Mary with their own intentions in their heart. Thanksgiving for her guidance, problems we needed help with, doubts in our faith, or just out of love. I came with my sister. I didn't know what her intention was, but I certainly knew mine. I prayed for our mother, who was very ill with heart disease.

For nine days we walked, to arrive on 15 August, the feast of the Assumption. Oh, the relief of reaching our destination. To fall into Our Mother's arms was beautiful. In Mary's presence, I prayed for my mother.

At Częstochowa, too, each day ended with the 9 p.m. hymn. 'O, Mary, Queen of Poland, I am with you, I remember, I keep vigil.' How lovely to sing it in her holy presence, finally! Each morning, the original icon, normally covered by a replica for protection, would be slowly unveiled to great fanfare and hymns. It often brought a tear to my eye. It was like watching a sunrise.

We came home, invigorated, and life went back to normal. About a month later my mother went to a doctor's appointment and came home, amazed. 'He says I am fine,' she exclaimed, 'No heart disease!' My sister and I looked at each other silently. We almost couldn't believe it, yet we knew miracles were possible. Our Lady had heard our prayers. My mother was healed.

After that first pilgrimage, I was hooked. Everyone came on the pilgrimage again the next year. And the next. I made the pilgrimage every year for seven years. I'll never forget the year it rained almost every day, for seven days. By day three everyone was so exasperated. You were walking, you were hungry, you were wet, but how could you eat? There was no shelter. You took your food out and it got wet. By day five you couldn't care less any more. 'Oh, still raining? Never mind, I'll just eat a wet sandwich.'

I learned everything I know about patience from those pilgrimages. Why worry? When problems come along now, even to this day, I just relax, pray, and don't worry. God will take care of it. If I had never been on pilgrimage I don't think I would have ever learned those valuable lessons. I practise them every day.

The pilgrimages also allowed me to experience charity in a wonderful new way. In the towns we passed, the locals would turn on their heaters in advance, knowing that we were coming, and welcome us into their homes to dry off and rest. At one supermarket they gave us all their plastic bags to hold off the rain. People were so generous.

Our Lady of Czestochowa always inspires the best in people. She loves us and protects us—a truly great Queen of Poland. I love to talk about her, even though people sometimes think I'm crazy!

I remember when I began working, one of my colleagues thought I was a bit weird. It was the mid '80s, and a great disaster happened in the Baltic Sea. A naval ship was sunk in an accident, and all of those on board died but one. I wondered if perhaps he had survived because he prayed to Our Lady. It was a very sad story, but I put it out of my mind.

About a week later, I happened to come across an interview with the mother of the survivor. She told a lovely story of how much she prayed when her son said he wanted to join the Navy. She took him to Czestochowa and entrusted him to Our Lady. When he left, she came to the shrine to pray every day. Suddenly I knew how he had managed to survive. I gave the article to one of my colleagues at work, and yes, he started to believe that maybe there was something to this Lady of Czestochowa thing!

Our Lady has always been here for me and never failed me. When I came to Australia ten years ago—with no English—she was right there by my side. I learned most of my English from a rosary group I joined. Now, when I go back to Poland, I always visit Jasna Góra. I see my family and friends, but no trip is complete without a visit to our Blessed Mother.

My favourite moment with Our Lady? Each moment is new and full of wonderful surprises! It seems each time I walk in to the chapel at Jasna Góra I arrive exactly on time for Mass, even when I don't plan it—a special gift from Our Lady. The last time, I walked in just in time for a special Mass for Polish expatriate families. It was lovely!

But I remember one year, when a group of us were given special permission to go beyond the metal gates that normally protect Our Lady. We spent the whole night before her in prayer. I had never been so close. I could have reached out and touched her! The whole night seemed to fly by. It was like being in heaven—I felt as if I was floating in air.

I have felt that many times. But faith is about more than just feelings, and I pray to Our Lady even when I don't feel like it. Being near Our Lady is like being near to heaven. Whether I'm in Jasna Góra or Australia, she is always close. She is known by many names in Poland and all over the world. She has many faces, but she is one Mother. I will always have a special place in my heart for our beautiful Lady of Czestochowa.

—Henryka, *Western Australia*

The Miraculous Medal of Mary
— France —

In 1806, in the little village of Fain-les-moutiers near Dijon in Burgundy, Catherine Labouré was born. Her father owned the largest farm in the village, so she and her ten brothers and sisters had a good life, until the death of their mother when Catherine was just nine years old.

In her grief, Catherine saw a statue of the Virgin Mary on a high shelf in her mother's bedroom and climbed a chair to reach it. 'Now, dear Blessed Mother,' she said, clasping it to her heart. 'You will be my mother.' From that moment, every time she faced doubt, fear or persecution, Catherine would hold Mary close to her heart.

Catherine and her younger sister Tonine were sent to live with a relative in the nearby village of Saint-Rémy. Here the local priest gave Catherine religious instruction. It was the closest Catherine would ever get to a formal education, though her parents and siblings had all received some schooling. Lack of education would prove a great handicap to Catherine for the rest of her life.

When her older sister entered a convent, Catherine, now twelve, was brought home to run the household. She cooked, cleaned and cared for the animals and workmen on the farm. She went to church as often as she could. Even when it meant long walks to the nearby village, no effort seemed too great for the hard-working country girl. It wasn't long before she felt a desire for religious life, but her father had already allowed one daughter to enter the convent and he did not want to lose another. She was sent to Paris to forget the idea, but this only deepened her longing. She finally became a novice with the Sisters of Charity in Châtillon, at the age of twenty-three. She was an unremarkable novice. Though intelligent, she had atrocious spelling, but she always worked hard, and kept to herself.

Her preferred companions were God and the saints. One night during her first year in the convent, she was given a relic of Saint Vincent de Paul, one of the founders of her order. It was a summer night, and the eve of the feast of St Vincent de Paul. Before she went to sleep that night she cut it in two and swallowed a piece, with a sincere prayer that Saint Vincent would grant her something she had long been praying for, the grace of seeing the Blessed Virgin who had guided her from childhood.

Near midnight, she was awoken by a voice calling her name. Catherine later recorded what happened next. 'I looked towards where the voice came from and, pulling my bed curtain aside, I saw a child of about four or five dressed in white. He said, "Come to the chapel. The Blessed Virgin is waiting for you." I thought that someone would hear me, but the child said to me, "Don't be uneasy. It is half past eleven, and everyone is asleep. So come, and don't be afraid. I'm waiting for you."

'I dressed hurriedly and went with the child. He was all radiant with light and walked on my left. I was very astonished to see all the lamps lit in the passage. I was even more astonished when the door of the chapel opened up at the mere touch of the child's finger, and I saw the chapel lit up as if for midnight Mass. But I did not see the Blessed Virgin.

'The child led me into the sanctuary. I knelt down by the side of the father director's chair. The child remained standing . . . At last, the moment arrived and the child warned me: "Here is the Blessed Virgin—here she is!" I heard a slight noise like the rustling of a silk dress coming from the side of the sanctuary where the picture of Saint Joseph hung.

The Blessed Virgin appeared and sat in the father director's chair. I looked at her, not knowing if she was really the Blessed Virgin.'

Here the child repeated his words, and Catherine understood who the visitor was. 'It is impossible to express what I felt then,' she continued. 'I hesitated no longer. I looked at her, took a step forward, fell on my knees on the altar steps and put my hands on her knees. There I enjoyed the sweetest moment of my life.'

Mary talked to Catherine of the future of France, foretelling the assassination of an archbishop of Paris, and the violent political disturbances still to come. The dramatic political upheavals came the following week, in the violent three-day revolution of July 1830. In 1848, Monseigneur Affre, Archbishop of Paris, was shot and killed as he attempted to bring peace to a rioting crowd.

'I have a mission to entrust to you,' Mary said. 'You will suffer much in its performance, but the thought that it will be for the glory of God will enable you to overcome all trials. You will be opposed, but do not be afraid. Grace will be given to you.'

'I do not know how long I stayed there,' wrote Catherine, 'but a moment came when she was no longer by me, and I saw her vanish like a shadow at the side of the sanctuary from which she came. I rose from the altar steps, absorbed in what I had seen and heard, and, turning around, I saw the child still standing there. All he said was, "She has gone."

'We turned to the dormitory along the same passage, which was still lit up. I believe the child was my guardian angel, because I had always prayed to him for the favour of seeing the Blessed Virgin. I heard the clock strike two as soon as I got back into bed, but I could not go to sleep again.'

Life returned to normal until 27 November, when Catherine and the other novices were in the chapel for evening meditation. They were praying in silence when Catherine's ears were awakened to a sound she'd heard before, the gentle swish of a silken gown.

Gazing up, she saw Mary standing beside an image of Joseph. Her golden white gown and veil floated to her feet, which rested on a globe. In her hands, she held a smaller globe, and she was looking up as if to the heavens. After a moment the small globe disappeared and Mary raised her hands towards Catherine. Jewelled rings seemed to appear on her fingers, emitting brilliant rays of light. The beams fell on her feet and the globe below. Catherine heard a voice some-where inside her.

'My child, this globe represents the world and France in particular and also every individual soul.' The voice explained that the lights from the rings were 'a symbol of the graces I shower on all who ask them of me'.

A great oval frame appeared, encircling Our Lady and the globe, and from her right hand to her left a curved line of words appeared: 'O Mary, conceived without sin, pray for us who have recourse to thee.'

The voice inside Catherine spoke again. 'Have a medal struck,' it said, 'according to this model.' Mary promised 'abundant graces for those who wore it with trust', especially if they wore it round the neck.

The image before Catherine seemed to turn, and another image appeared: a great letter M, entwined in a cross. Beneath this were two hearts, one pierced by a sword, the other by a crown of thorns. Then the image vanished, along with Mary, and the bewildered Catherine was left to her own private thoughts. The other novices had seen nothing.

Catherine poured her heart out to her confessor, Father Aladel. A prudent man, he did nothing to encourage her. After all, there was every chance that she was delusional, or at the very least overimaginative. He would wait and see.

The next month, as she meditated in the chapel, Catherine saw Mary again. This time, the rustling sound came from the high altar, above and behind the tabernacle. At Mary's feet was a serpent. On her hands, some of her brilliant gemstones had become dull. They were 'the graces people forget to ask for', she explained sadly.

'You know very well that Father Aladel does not believe me,' Catherine said to Mary. 'He will not have your medal struck.'

'Don't worry,' Mary reassured her, 'One day he will do what I want. He is my servant, and is afraid of displeasing me.' Catherine went back to her doubting confessor and told him all that had happened. This time Father Aladel asked the Archbishop of Paris for permission to have the medals struck. He agreed, and an initial 1500 medals were produced. Reports of special graces and miracles began to come in from all over France. Wearing the medal, combined with earnest prayer, produced some marvellous results. Demand for the medals grew. In the following decade, one Parisian factory alone produced twenty million medals.

In 1836, four years after the first medals were made, the Church held an inquiry into the apparitions. The report to the archbishop concluded: 'If the medal came into being through lies and trickery, heaven would not allow it to be the source of the graces and favours which have been and are being showered on those who have faith in it.'

Catherine Labouré continued her own humble work, quietly and anonymously, while the world was swept with enthusiasm for the medal and gratitude for the grace that flowed from it. No one knew who she was, let alone what she had done. She lived an unassuming life of service, spending forty-five years in the Hospice d'Enghien caring for poor and elderly men, working in the kitchen and laundry, answering the door. At the age of seventy, she died, as she had lived, in obscurity.

In 1933, Catherine's body was exhumed from the hospice chapel. It showed no signs of decay. Fourteen years later she was declared a saint. Now Saint Catherine's body lies in the chapel at Rue du Bac, where her dream to see Mary had come true.

Receive this holy medal, wear it faithfully and treat it with due veneration, so that the most pious and Immaculate Queen of Heaven may protect and defend thee, and, ever renewing the wonders of her goodness, may mercifully obtain for thee whatever thou humbly ask of God: that thou may rest happily in her maternal embrace throughout life and in death. Amen.
—DEDICATION OF THE MIRACULOUS MEDAL

The Madonna of the Miracle
— France —

Marie-Alphonse Ratisbonne was born into a wealthy Jewish family of bankers. When his older brother converted to Catholicism and became a priest, the family disowned and disinherited him. Young Marie-Alphonse vowed never to speak to his brother again.

Ratisbonne studied law and was something of an intellectual. He was not an observant Jew; instead he declared himself to be agnostic. At twenty-eight, newly engaged and seeking a last bachelor's fling, he set off for a winter holiday around Europe. But on the way he took a wrong turn and ended up on a ship to Rome.

Deciding to make the most of it, he set out to explore the city, including Rome's notorious Jewish ghetto. The squalor and poverty only increased his hostility towards Christianity.

On his wanderings, Ratisbonne ran into an old Protestant classmate from Strasburg. He introduced Ratisbonne to his older brother, the Baron Theodore de Bussières, a Catholic convert who happened to be a close friend of Ratisbonne's long-lost priest–brother.

Ratisbonne was not keen on Catholics but he planned to visit Constantinople, and the baron was an expert on the city. So he agreed to visit him. Somehow the two overcame their religious differences and became friends.

The baron believed that the power of Mary could soften Ratisbonne's heart. So he issued a challenge: wear the miraculous medal and recite the Memorare, a short prayer to the Mother of

God, every morning. Seeing this as an opportunity to expose Catholicism as superstitious nonsense, Ratisbonne agreed. 'If it does me no good, at least it will do me no harm,' he laughed, bending to let the baron's little daughter hang the medal around his neck. The baron, meanwhile, asked other aristocratic French expatriates living in Rome to pray for Ratisbonne.

One of them was the ex-diplomat Count Laferronays. After a notoriously wild and scandalous youth, he was now a devout Catholic. He prayed more than twenty Memorares for Ratisbonne's conversion. The same evening, he suffered a heart attack and died.

The sad news spread fast. The baron and Ratisbonne went to the Basilica of St Andrea delle Fratte, where Ratisbonne waited while his friend made funeral arrangements. When he returned to Ratisbonne, the baron found him on his knees, weeping.

All the way back to the hotel, Ratisbonne kept weeping and clutching the miraculous medal around his neck, murmuring his thanks to God. Finally he embraced the baron and begged to be taken to a priest.

'What has happened?' cried the baron. 'What have you seen?' But Ratisbonne would tell him nothing. The baron took Ratisbonne to a house of Jesuit priests. Still in tears and grasping the medal, he cried, 'I saw her. I saw her . . . She spoke not a word, but I understood all.'

He went on to tell an astonishing tale. 'I was scarcely in the church,' he explained, 'when a total confusion came over me. When I looked up, it seemed to me that the entire church had been swallowed up in shadow, except one chapel. It was as though all the light was concentrated in that single place. I looked over towards this chapel whence so much light shone, and above the altar was a living figure, tall, majestic, beautiful and full of mercy.

'It was the most Holy Virgin Mary, resembling her figure on the miraculous medal. At this sight I fell on my knees right where I stood. Unable to look up because of the blinding light, I fixed my glance on her hands, and in them I could read the expression of mercy and pardon. In the presence of the Most Blessed Virgin, even though she did not speak a word to me, I understood the frightful situation I was in, my sins and the beauty of the Catholic faith.' Eleven days later, he was baptised.

Ratisbonne's story soon spread, and many gathered to witness the baptism. A lengthy Vatican investigation concluded that the sudden conversion was entirely miraculous, an act of God made possible through the powerful help of the Virgin. The conversion of Ratisbonne spread devotion to the miraculous medal beyond France to the world.

An image of the apparition was painted and placed in the spot where Mary had appeared. It was given the name the Madonna of the Miracle. Ratisbonne immediately reconciled with his priest–brother and helped him found the Sisterhood of Our Lady of Sion, a religious order that cared for Jews and worked and prayed for their conversion. He himself became a Jesuit priest. He eventually went with the Sisters of Sion to Jerusalem, where he built convents, schools and orphanages and continued working towards the conversion of Jews and Muslims. When he died he reportedly went into ecstasy as he saw, one last time, the holy lady who had led him to conversion.

Remember, O most gracious Virgin Mary,
That never was it known
That anyone who fled to your protection, implored your help
Or sought your intercession was left unaided.

Inspired with confidence, I fly to you, O Virgin of virgins,
    my mother.
To you I come, before you I stand, sinful and sorrowful.
O Mother of the Word Incarnate, despise not my petitions,
But in your mercy, hear and answer me.
Amen.

—MEMORARE PRAYER

Mary of Light
— Egypt —

Just after sunset on an early April evening in 1968, thousands of eyes were drawn to the domes of the Virgin Mary Orthodox Coptic Church in Zeitoun, Cairo. The shining figure of a woman in white was hovering in the air among the rooftops. A halo of white light surrounded her head, and doves of white light flew about her as she moved. Fragrant purple smoke filled the air. For three hours, people watched the strange and beautiful figure, and miraculous healings took place in the crowd.

A resident of Tumanbay Street, where the church stands, still remembers that first apparition: 'There used to be a big garage for public buses opposite the church, and an hour and a half after sunset, the mechanics and drivers of the garage [who were Muslims] were alarmed by a disturbance in the street. They ran outside and looked in the direction of the raised faces of the people. A young woman dressed in white had appeared on the church dome. They saw her moving on it and thought that she was about to throw herself off. "Be careful, take care, you may fall! Wait!" they cried, before they realised that the dome was curved and that no human being could walk on it. Then some of the people watching cried out, "The Virgin Mary, the Virgin Mary!" The traffic in Tumanbay Street stopped and the crowd grew bigger and bigger. The whole street was closed and public buses were not allowed to pass through. People would come and spend the night in the garage opposite the church.'

This was only the first of many similar apparitions over the next four years, which would last anywhere from several minutes to nine hours at a time. They were broadcast live on Egyptian television and were witnessed by millions of Egyptians and visitors, people of no faith and all faiths—Orthodox, Catholics, Protestants, Muslims, Jews. Even the Egyptian president, Gamal Abdel Nasser, witnessed the phenomenon. After he saw that people were sleeping in the nearby garage waiting for the apparition, he gave the land to the Church so it could be turned into a cathedral.

At first the local police assumed the apparition of Mary was some kind of hoax. They scoured the streets around the church for twenty-five kilometres but failed to discover any device that could have produced the images. When the electricity was cut off in the area, the apparition shone even brighter. Healings continued and were verified by doctors. Blindness, muteness, paralysis and cancer were just some of the disorders that were miraculously cured.

The lady would appear kneeling in prayer before a shining cross, surrounded by white stars or waving and nodding in a gesture of blessing. Sometimes she appeared in full form, sometimes in a bust. At other times she appeared as a very bright cloud, surrounded by dove-shaped lights moving at high speed. On occasion an angel would appear behind her, spreading his wings, or tongues of yellowish flame would flash above the church. Now and then she would seem to be holding an olive branch, a sign of peace and a symbol of the town of Zeitoun, named after the Arabic word for olives.

Pope Kyrillos VI, the Coptic Orthodox patriarch, launched a commission to investigate the apparitions, and just over a month after the first sighting, he confirmed them as miraculous. The local Catholic patriarch, the head of all Protestant evangelical ministries in Egypt, and the head of the Jesuit college all agreed: this was indeed *Sitt Mariam*, Saint Mary. All those who saw Mary honoured her in their own ways. Some wept, some were healed, all prayed.

These silent apparitions left devotees to form their own conclusions. One possible explanation lies in the origins of the Coptic church itself. The lovely, domed church was built in 1924 on the site where Christians believed Mary, Joseph and the infant Jesus lived after they fled from Roman persecution in Jerusalem. According to local legend, the Virgin Mary had appeared to the son of a prosperous lawyer, asking him to build a church in her name on that spot. She vowed to appear again fifty years from that day, and fulfilled her promise on 2 April 1968.

One historian of the event, Pearl Zaki, suggested that Mary's appearance so soon after the Six-Day War between the Arabs and Israel was a call to peace. As Copts could no longer visit the holy places of Jerusalem, perhaps Mary had come to them. Or perhaps her appearance was in answer to the prayers of Arab Christians in Egypt, Lebanon and Syria.

Despite their differences, the Muslims and Christians of Zeitoun joined in a deep respect and reverence for the apparition. People would stand from evening until morning, praying and singing hymns in the streets surrounding the church.

In Zeitoun, Mary reached out personally to Muslims, first appearing to Muslim mechanics and drivers working at the Public Transport Authority opposite the church. A Muslim mechanic was the first to be miraculously healed. His finger was scheduled to be amputated the next day, but when his bandages were removed for the operation his wounds had vanished.

Mary, or *Maryam*, as she is known in Arabic, is the only woman named in the Qu'ran. It has a chapter named after her, and describes her life in more detail than the Bible. While the two books differ on important details, they both emphasise Mary's purity, faithfulness and service to God.

Wagih Rizk, a professional photographer who had lost the use of his left arm in a car accident the year before, heard about the apparitions in Zeitoun and felt compelled to visit the church. He saw Mary for the first time at 2.45 in the morning. She was radiating an almost blinding light. 'The apparition was awesome . . . Reverence and fear filled me like an electric shock,' he recalls. Unable to sleep after this life-changing event, he was seized with the desire to photograph the vision, but on subsequent visits either Mary failed to appear or Wagih was too awestruck to move in her presence. Finally, at 3.40 a.m. on 13 April he took some shots and returned home in great excitement, unable to sleep.

'I recalled in my mind every moment that passed while the Virgin was appearing in front of me . . . I forgot while I was looking at the apparition of the Blessed Virgin the fact that when I captured the first photo quickly, I used my left hand! Yes, my left hand . . . the hand five doctors, some of them are among the most famous surgeons in Egypt, said was hopeless and will never move again . . . the Virgin Mary has miraculously healed this hand! I started to move my left hand, up, down, to my side, and to rotate it and wave it in the air while extended . . . I was cured . . . completely cured once the Virgin appeared. And from this day the camera never leaves me, and the camera and I never leave Zeitoun.'

Wagih Rizik never sold the photos or charged anyone for publishing them. The apparitions ended in 1971, after the Egyptian government was said to have started selling tickets to see Mary.

Zeitoun was the first place in Egypt to be graced with apparitions of Mary, but it certainly wasn't the last. Egypt seems to be a country that is close to Mary's heart. The Coptic Christian Church in Egypt relates a detailed history of Mary's journey in Egypt with Joseph and the infant Jesus. In many of the places they visited miracles followed. Since Mary's appearances at Zeitoun, miraculous apparitions have been reported at all these sites.

One of Mary's gifts to the world is peace. This has certainly been the case in Egypt. Since Mary appeared in Assiut, a hotbed of religious division, Christian–Muslim relations have greatly improved.

Mary still makes her presence felt in Zeitoun through the new sense of community that has developed around her church. A new cathedral has been constructed opposite the domed church. Around it are two homes for the elderly, a hostel for young female pilgrims and students from outside Cairo, and a clinic where the poor receive free medical treatment. The church also ensures that the needy receive legal advice, the unemployed are given work opportunities, and students are given financial aid. It provides everything from blankets for the destitute to counselling and spiritual guidance. Now people come from all over the world to Zeitoun to pray. More than 4000 people typically attend Masses there on Fridays and Sundays. In this troubled area of the world, Mary, the Mother of Light, comes to all her children, guiding them in her own, gentle, quiet path of reconciliation.

Mary, God has chosen thee. And purified thee;
He has chosen thee. Above all women.
—FROM THE QU'RAN, A VERSE CHANTED BY THE MUSLIM FAITHFUL
AS THEY WATCHED THE APPARITION OF MARY IN ZEITOUN

O Theotokos [Mother of God], the second Heaven,
You are the honoured Mother of the Light.
—FROM THE COPTIC ORTHODOX BOOK OF HOURS

Mary in Egypt

The entire Egyptian nation is adorned with places where Mary travelled with Joseph and Jesus during their escape from Herod. Oral tradition records three and a half difficult years in which the holy family moved through Egypt seeking refuge from Roman persecution.

According to the Coptic Orthodox Church, their path was chronicled by the Coptic Pope Theophilus four centuries later, when Our Lady appeared to him and revealed details of their journey. Today, wells, churches and springs are held sacred as places where the family stopped and rested. At Mostorod, once called Al Mahamma, the 'bathing place', Mary stopped to bathe Jesus and clean his clothes. At Wadi Natroun, amidst a cluster of salt lakes, the one freshwater well is known as Beer Mariam, Mary's Well.

In Matariyah, in what is today a suburb of Cairo, the Virgin Mary washed Jesus' clothes and poured the water in the ground. A fragrant balsam tree grew on the spot—a tree foreign to Egyptian soil. The holy family rested in its shade. Essence of balsam is used in healing and in the preparation of perfumes for the holy oil used in Coptic ceremonies. The tree still stands today, the site of many pilgrimages, and is known as St Mary's Tree.

Mary of Lourdes
— France —

In the village of Lourdes, in the picturesque mountains of the Pyrénées in southwestern France, the Soubirous family were the lowest of the low. The father, an unsuccessful miller, had been imprisoned for petty theft and the family was forced to move out of their mill. Their new home was a single room in a run-down building that had formerly been the local jail. It retained the atmosphere of a prison, with its single barred window and few pieces of furniture.

On a clear February morning in 1858, fourteen-year-old Bernadette Soubirous went with her sister Toinette and their friend Jeanne to collect firewood. Winter was beginning to fade from the French countryside, but in the shade of the towering mountains the three girls felt a stinging chill in the air.

As they wandered, they came to a shallow canal that flowed into the River Gave, trickling amid the grey, craggy stones known as the rocks of Massabielle. Toinette and Jeanne wasted no time stripping off their wooden clogs and wading into the clear water, squealing playfully.

Bernadette, a sickly child, was more reserved. She asked Toinette to throw some stones into the canal so she could step across in a more ladylike fashion. Instead the two younger girls crossed the stream and continued into the woods, chatting happily, and went thoughtlessly on their way.

Left alone on the other side, Bernadette had little choice but to follow. Taking off her stockings and sabots, she poked a tentative foot into the water. Suddenly a sound roared past her, like a great gust of wind—except that the poplar trees on the river's edge remained motionless. Another similar sound drew her eyes across the stream to a wild rose bush growing among some prickly brambles. It marked the entrance to a yawning cave.

In the opening was the shining figure of a young girl. She wore a simple white gown tied with a blue sash. On each bare foot was a single yellow rose, and on her head she wore a veil. Her arms were outstretched as if to embrace Bernadette, and a rosary dangled from her wrist. The young woman glowed with a light that Bernadette described as brighter than any she'd seen, but it didn't hurt her eyes or disorient her. Bernadette noticed that she was taller than the girl, who appeared to be about her own age.

Bernadette fell to her knees and took out her rosary beads, but could not pray or move her hand. When the girl raised her own hand to make the sign of the cross, Bernadette realised she was free to do the same. As Bernadette prayed on each bead, the light-filled young girl passed her own beads through her fingers, as though they were praying in unison, but without words. As Bernadette's prayer drew to an end, the girl bowed her head and vanished.

Toinette and Jeanne returned to find Bernadette on her knees. She seemed oblivious to their shouts and to the pebbles her sister threw at her to attract her attention. Toinette feared for a moment that she was dead, but Bernadette soon rose and crossed the stream to join her friends. 'What fibbers you are,' she cried cheerfully. 'Fancy saying the water's cold. It's as warm as washing-up water.'

Arriving at the other side, Bernadette asked the girls if they had seen anything. 'No,' they replied, puzzled. 'What have you seen?'

'Nothing,' said Bernadette dismissively. But she could not put her encounter out of her mind.

When Jeanne left for home Bernadette confided the story to her sister and made her promise to tell no one. But when they arrived home Toinette told everything to their mother, Louise, the moment Bernadette left the room.

Bernadette returned to a very hostile mother. Louise questioned her harshly and beat both girls with a stick. She tried to convince Bernadette that she had only seen a white stone, but Bernadette clung faithfully to her story. Louise forbade Bernadette to go to the cave again.

Three days later, however, an inner prompting took Bernadette to the grotto once more. Again the beautiful figure appeared, blessing Bernadette with a sprinkling of holy water. Without saying a word, she smiled while Bernadette prayed the rosary, then vanished.

The story of the apparitions began to spread. A few days later, Bernadette returned to the grotto very early in the morning. With her came two women, bearing a consecrated candle, pen, paper and ink. As the young girl appeared once more, Bernadette found courage to speak. 'If you come from God, please tell me what you want. If not, go away.'

Mary smiled at these discerning words, then shook her head. Bernadette took it as sign that she should leave and began to back away. Mary indicated that she should stay and sent away the two women. They moved back, though they had seen nothing.

'Will you please write down your name, what you want?' asked Bernadette.

Mary smiled as she replied in Bernadette's local dialect, 'There is no need to write down what I have to say to you.'

In great excitement, Bernadette ran to tell the other two what the radiant girl had said. Mary laughed to see her joy. When she returned, Mary asked, 'Will you do me the favour of coming here for a fortnight?'

Bernadette was thrilled at the prospect of seeing this lovely vision so often, and would have loved to cry 'Yes!' straightaway, but, remembering her mother's stern disapproval, she promised she would come if she could obtain her parents' permission.

'I do not promise to make you happy in this world,' Mary said, 'but in the next.' And she vanished.

Bernadette's parents did give their consent, and for the next fourteen days Bernadette would be drawn to the holy grotto, often followed by curious, ever-growing crowds. Despite their excitement, Bernadette's only concern would be for the beautiful girl Mary. Sometimes she would speak; other times they would gaze silently at each other.

As the next day was Good Friday, the day of Christ's death on the Cross, Bernadette came to the grotto with a lighted, priest-blessed candle, beginning a tradition that is still observed at Lourdes today. On this occasion, too, no words were exchanged. It was simply a moment of peace.

During one appearance, Mary taught Bernadette a personal prayer that left the peasant girl feeling sad. Another time, she told her a secret that was for her alone.

But it was the ninth apparition that would leave its most lasting effect on the community of Lourdes. About 300 people had gathered around the grotto. Though they could neither see nor hear Mary, they knew they were in the presence of something remarkable.

When Mary appeared, she told Bernadette to enter the grotto on her knees. She pointed to the earth. 'Go and drink and wash at the spring, and eat some of the green material you find growing there.' Bernadette thought she must mean the River Gave, but as she was turning to go there Mary stopped her. Bernadette looked at Mary's still pointing finger, and realised she was indicating a puddle of murky water. Dropping to her knees, she scooped up the earth.

The first three handfuls of water were too muddy, but at the fourth attempt she was able to drink. She washed her hands and her face, leaving muddy streaks down her cheeks. She found some bitter herbs near the puddle, which she ate at Mary's bidding. By now many of the watching crowd had left, convinced that this 'visionary' was mad.

By the next day, the puddle had turned into a trickle. That day's Mass readings spoke of 'a pool in Jerusalem . . . under which a multitude of distressed folk used to lie, the blind, the lame, the disabled, waiting for a disturbance of the water. From time to time, an angel of the Lord came down upon the pool, and the water was stirred up; and the first man who stepped into the pool after the stirring of the water, recovered from whatever infirmity it was that oppressed him.'

In hindsight, it seems to predict the future of that little spring in the grotto, and the grace that would flow along with its water. The puddle itself was not a miracle. There had always been a trickle of water in the grotto, from an ancient underground water source. The ground in the grotto was cleared, and after some excavations the water flowed abundantly, with over 100,000 litres spilling forth each day. It seemed strange that Mary had encouraged Bernadette to rediscover this long-ignored spring.

Over the next few days the inner calling drew Bernadette repeatedly to the grotto. Sometimes she would wash at the spring or enter reverently on her knees, praying and kissing the ground in dramatic acts of reverence. She was interrogated, threatened with imprisonment, harassed by crowds, but her only interest was in remaining faithful to Mary.

Three days after the discovery of the spring, the first miraculous healing was reported at Lourdes. That night Bernadette's friend, Catherine Latapie, slipped into the grotto and plunged her painful dislocated arm into the water. When she pulled it out, her arm and hand could move again.

The already huge crowds seemed to double overnight. Mary told Bernadette, 'Go, tell the priests to come here in procession and to build a chapel here.'

Bernadette went faithfully to Father Peyramale, the parish priest of Lourdes, to report what Mary had said. But he wasn't inclined to obey some mysterious figure in a cave that inspired odd behaviour and outlandish stories. He wanted to know the figure's identity. If she was Mary she should prove it with a miracle, making the wild roses at the grotto bloom in the middle of winter.

Next morning Bernadette arrived at the grotto bright and early, accompanied by an estimated 3000 people. No figure appeared. She went to school, but it wasn't until the end of the day that she felt the familiar inner voice again. Bernadette went to the grotto and found Mary there. Again she asked for her name. She was answered only with a benevolent smile. Returning to Father Peyramale, she faced the same straight response: 'If she really wishes that a chapel be built, then she must tell us her name and make the rose bush bloom at the grotto.'

When Bernadette returned to the grotto, she found that the wild rose bush remained flowerless. Mary had a more unique way of letting herself be known, as Bernadette later recalled. 'She lifted up her eyes to heaven, joined her hands as though in prayer, and holding them out and open towards the ground she said to me: "I am the Immaculate Conception."'

Bernadette ran from the grotto, calling out, '*Immaculada Concepciou! Immaculada Concepciou!*'

Unbeknown to Bernadette, this was a controversial title which had been conferred on the Virgin Mary just four years before. It meant that Mary was born without original sin, and after much scholarly and theological debate Pope Pius IX had declared this as dogma, a fundamental truth of the Catholic faith. When he heard these words, the doubting priest knew that Bernadette had seen Mary.

On 16 July, the feast of Our Lady of Mount Carmel, Mary made her final appearance. Finding her path to the grotto barred by barricades set up by local authorities, Bernadette went to the other side of the River Gave and knelt there, gazing across at the grotto. 'I felt that I was in front of the grotto, at the same distance as before,' she said later. 'I saw only the Blessed Virgin, and she was more beautiful than ever!'

The grotto quickly became a place of pilgrimage. While civil authorities bickered over how to handle the crowds, the Catholic Church launched into a detailed investigation that would last for almost four years. In 1862 Monseigneur Laurence, the Bishop of Tarbes and Lourdes, announced that a miracle had indeed occurred at Lourdes. A great Gothic basilica was erected in response to Our Lady's request for a chapel.

Bernadette became greatly esteemed for her faithfulness to Mary. 'Who could not admire, on meeting her, the simplicity, the openness, and the modesty of this child?' observed the Bishop of Tarbes and Lourdes. 'She only spoke when she was spoken to. She spoke without exaggeration and with a touching naivety. To the many questions asked of her, she gave clear and precise answers, always to the point, without hesitation and stamped with a strong conviction.'

Bernadette was placed in the care of the Sisters of Charity at Nevers, where she was taught to read and write. After her experiences with Mary, Bernadette began to feel drawn to a simple life of prayer as a nun. At the age of twenty-two she joined the Sisters of Nevers because unlike other religious houses, 'they did not try to attract me,' she later said.

Taking the name Sister Marie-Bernard, she lived there until her feeble health finally claimed her at the age of thirty-five. A sister once asked her if she suffered from pride, for being the chosen messenger of Mary. 'How can I?' she answered. 'The Blessed Virgin chose me only because I was the most ignorant.'

On her deathbed, Bernadette's final words were a prayer to Mary. The Church later recognised her as a saint.

Today Lourdes is one of the largest and most famous pilgrimage sites in the world. People come from everywhere seeking cures and miracles, and all are welcomed and cared for.

Many bathe in the waters of Lourdes, as Bernadette once washed at the tiny puddle in the grotto. Sometimes unexplained physical healings are reported, more often people arrive at a sense of profound peace. It seems Mary is still present at Lourdes.

O brilliant star of sanctity, as on that lovely day, upon a rough rock in Lourdes you spoke to the child Bernadette and a fountain broke from the plain earth and miracles happened and the great shrine of Lourdes began, so now I beseech you to hear our fervent prayer.

—Novena prayer to Our Lady of Lourdes

My Change of Heart

Fifteen years ago I was a nominal Catholic. I believed in God even though to me he was a distant God. I don't quite know how I came to think like that. I went to Mass, but to me it was just something you did on Sundays with your children. I had three children at that stage, but I wasn't a satisfied person, I was just drifting on.

During a conversation with a friend about my unfulfilled life, she told me she prayed when things were not going right. My response was, well, God knows everything and he will help me if he chooses to. I didn't think it was up to me to tell him what I wanted. I went home and did nothing. A few days later I had a dream and saw a person I now recognise as Our Lady, with four cherubic angels: two above her, one on each side of her head, two at about knee height, one on either side. Our Lady was clasping her hands as if in prayer, indicating to me to pray. It seemed like she was saying to me without words: 'Pray, pray, pray.'

When I woke up, I immediately thought of the dream and I felt compelled to say the rosary, even though I had not done that for over twenty years. I didn't even own rosary beads. My friend told me to go to the church, where I would find people who would pray it with me, so I went. It was after weekday Mass, and there were people there praying the rosary. I couldn't bring myself to join them, so I sat at the back of the church and felt a stranger in my own parish. I responded to the Hail Mary prayers, reciting whatever bits I could remember.

After the rosary I was looking at the notice board to see where I could buy beads when my eyes fell on a poster advertising an oratorio that was coming up at the parish. I didn't know what that was but I felt I had to attend. The day came, and I went along. The church was packed, and there were people up on the sanctuary, men and women dressed in black and white. I realised I was also wearing a black skirt and white top. I was dressed just like them. How embarrassing!

The singing was beautiful. I enjoyed every minute of it. At the end of their performance the music master announced that they were always looking for people to join their choir. I wanted to go up to him, but I didn't have the courage. I was standing there on my own, thinking about the invitation to join, when I felt a tap on my shoulder. I turned round and saw a lady in black and white. She asked me if I would like to join the choir, and without hesitation I said yes!

The following week, I went along to the rehearsal. I felt so much at home. They were a group of Catholic charismatics and they prayed and worshipped before the rehearsal. They were going to perform an oratorio at a conference in Walsingham. I felt I had to go with them, so I did. By the end of the conference I had come to know and fall in love with Our Lord and Saviour, Jesus Christ, at the replica of the home where Our Lady had lived with him.

Ten years after my first visit to Walsingham, I was asked to help with the sick on a pilgrimage to Lourdes, and I accepted. Lourdes is just amazing! I had a chance to take a sick person to the pools where people are immersed for healing. I was asked if I wanted to go in as well and I said yes. I was asked to pray for anything I wanted. I prayed for all the sick people I had seen in Lourdes. As I was being helped into the pool, my eyes fell on the statue of Our Lady at the end of the pool. I just ran to the statue and held on to it, crying.

I could not let go of it. I felt warm and comfortable holding on to it. I did not want to be pulled away from it and I couldn't stop crying. Eventually I was taken back into the changing room, still crying and overwhelmed by what had just happened.

A lady came over and told me to go and sit at the grotto and pray. I went and sat there and it felt like Our Lady saying to me, it's all right to have a statue, that she is not in the statue, but it's OK to pray before her statue. I had always been against religious statues and been quite vocal about it, but now Our Lady was explaining it to me, I had to laugh. Now I love statues of Our Lady. My favourite one is Our Lady of Grace.

I was thinking about my experiences in Walsingham and Lourdes, when suddenly I connected the two. It was Our Lady all along. She led me to Walsingham and then to Lourdes. I am glad she did it like that. I love her so much, she is my mother forever.

—Joana, *England*

Mary of the Word
— Rwanda —

It was late November in 1981, a little after midday, and the children were gathered in the dining room of Kibeho's small Catholic school, run by Rwandan Benebikira nuns. Sixteen-year-old Alphonsine was a quiet and sensible girl, well regarded by her teachers. Suddenly she heard a gentle voice calling, 'My daughter.'

Following the strange voice out to the corridor, she saw the figure of a beautiful barefooted woman. She wore a seamless white dress and veil. Her hands were clasped on her breast, and her fingers pointed to the sky. 'Who are you?' asked Alphonsine in amazement. '*Ndi Nyina wa Jambo*,' the beautiful woman replied. 'I am the Mother of the Word' (Jesus).

Alphonsine was mesmerised by the incandescent figure before her. To think that the heavenly queen had chosen to walk down her school hallway! It was more than she could take in. All she could do was gaze at the figure. Then Mary addressed her again, asking her whom she loved.

Without hesitating Alphonsine replied that she loved God and his mother Mary, who gave the world Jesus. At this response the radiant figure beamed. 'I have come to calm you because I have heard your prayers,' said Mary sweetly, adding, 'I would like your friends to have faith, because they do not believe strongly enough.' Mary spoke to Alphonsine in perfect Kinyarwanda, the local Rwandan language.

Alphonsine recited a few simple prayers and watched in amazement as Nyina wa Jambo departed, rising to heaven.

Alphonsine stood in the hallway without moving for a quarter of an hour. All attempts to budge her or provoke any response were in vain. No one believed in her 'apparition'.

As Alphonsine was a good student and a pious girl, her teachers supposed that she had been gripped by some kind of illness, and hoped it would pass. But the 'illness' took hold of Alphonsine again the very next evening. This time Mary appeared to her in her room in the dormitory. When Mary did appear in public, she would do so in the school yard or in an area that had been converted into a chapel. Later Alphonsine described her visitor as '. . . not white, as she is usually seen in holy pictures. I could not determine the colour of her skin, but she was of incomparable beauty.'

Mary continued to appear almost every Saturday, but only Alphonsine could see her. Curious schoolmates and teachers gathered to watch, and pilgrims began to come from beyond Kibeho. When Alphonsine fell into ecstasy, people would try to burn her with a match or prick her with a pin to provoke a reaction and expose her as a fraud. She remained oblivious to their efforts but not to their taunts and teasing. She was, after all, still an ordinary teenager. The opinions of her friends and peers meant a lot to her. 'People say that we are crazy,' Alphonsine confided to Nyina wa Jambo in their moments together.

Even though it was hard being mocked, Alphonsine continued to bear it patiently. It was a small price to pay for the joy she received from her visitor. On many occasions the students brought rosary beads to be blessed by Mary. They handed them to Alphonsine, and she would lift them to the Virgin for her blessing. As there were often several rosaries mixed up together, and Alphonsine was in a trance-like state when they were handed to her, she had no idea whose beads she was holding. When Mary appeared, her comforting face was all Alphonsine could see, and her words were the only sound she heard.

On one occasion Alphonsine was handed a set of beads that she was unable to lift. After the apparition passed, the students realised who they belonged to—a student who believed that Alphonsine's claims of seeing Mary were false.

Other strange events followed. A star and bright lights were observed in the students' dormitory where Nyina wa Jambo sometimes appeared. Pilgrims saw the sun and stars dancing in the sky for several minutes, or watched them disappear entirely, to be replaced by a greenish moon. At other times glowing crosses could be seen in the heavens. In January and February 1982, mysterious and frightening phenomena also appeared in the dormitory. Certain that it wasn't caused by Nyina wa Jambo, the nuns used holy water from Lourdes to drive it away. Although this worked, the holy water ran out, so they told Alphonsine to ask Mary to bless more water for them.

All this made life complicated for Alphonsine. As the only visionary, she was besieged by requests for explanations, accusations of fraud and pleas for miracles. Mary now frequently appeared in the school chapel during evening prayers, taking the opportunity to talk to the students through Alphonsine. These meetings were for the children only. Mary advised, encouraged, and gently guided the students, and many came to believe. But still there were doubters. Many girls felt that if only others could see Mary too, the apparitions would be credible to everyone. Mary responded simply, 'Pray yourselves to obtain this favour.' The favour was granted almost two months later.

Nathalie Mukamazimpaka was a devout seventeen-year-old who had been praying to Mary since she was a child. One evening she was in the school dormitory when a beautiful woman appeared and called, 'Nathalie, my child!' With delight and amazement, the girl replied, 'I am.'

'Pray, pray a lot,' the lady begged her, 'because the world is bad. Come. Love what is from heaven more than that of earth, because earthly things pass away quickly. You will find many sufferings in life.' The words were strong and clear.

'Wake up, stand up,' Mary said. 'Wash yourselves and look up attentively. We must dedicate ourselves to prayer; we must develop the virtues of charity, availability and humility. Return to God, the source of living water.'

Nathalie later described Mary as 'a living person, with an extraordinary beauty, neither black nor white. Her skin is very beautiful and soft.' She also spoke of her quiet, gentle voice. 'I received the message, the mission, like a grace,' she recalled in 2006. 'This grace is nevertheless accompanied by the cross. But joy and the cross aren't separate. I am happy, and I always ask the grace to hold on in this mission. I also received the grace to grow in the love of God, the Holy Virgin and my neighbour.' Nyina wa Jambo continued to visit Nathalie for almost two years.

At first Nathalie thought the lady was a saint. The radiant stranger revealed her name on the second evening. She explained that she was Mary, Nyina wa Jambo.

Alphonsine was delighted. At last she was no longer the lone visionary. And there was soon a third.

Nyina wa Jambo's next appearance was to Marie-Claire Mukangango, a girl who had called Alphonsine a fool. The outspoken twenty-one-year-old had never believed in the apparitions, and wasn't afraid to say so. Unlike Alphonsine and Nathalie, Marie-Claire was lukewarm in her faith, with little interest in anything spiritual. But once chosen, she was transformed.

In fifteen apparitions, from March to December 1982, Nyina wa Jambo told her that the world had turned against God. People needed to recognise this and ask for forgiveness.

Nyina wa Jambo once said to Alphonsine, 'If I am now turning to the parish of Kibeho it does not mean that I am concerned only for Kibeho . . . or for the whole of Africa,' she once told Alphonsine. 'I am concerned with and turning to the whole world.'

Mary encouraged the trio to pray, fast and do penance, but their encounters with her were joyful experiences, so much so that the girls sometimes danced. 'Although I am the Mother of God, I am simple and humble,' Mary said to Alphonsine. 'I always place myself where you are. I love you as you are. I never reproach my little ones. When a child is without reproach in front of her mother, she will tell her everything that is in her heart. I am grateful when a child of mine is joyful with me. That joy is a most beautiful sign of trust and love.

'Few understand the mysteries of God's love. Let me, as your mother, embrace all my children with love, so that you can confide your deepest longings to me. Know that I give all your longings to my son Jesus, your brother.'

Mary's extraordinary visits brought the three girls together. 'Often in the private apparitions, Alphonsine, Marie-Claire and I had visions on the same day,' Nathalie later said. 'Sometimes we prayed together, we discussed the messages that the Holy Virgin gave us.'

Within a few months the faithful and the curious from all over Africa were gathering in the schoolyard in the hope of glimpsing a miracle. The words of the seer were amplified by a speaker system. The media covered the story enthusiastically, and medical and theological commissions investigated the girls' claims. At one August gathering an estimated 20,000 people were present.

At the end of one of her visits, Mary told the seers to bless the crowd. But in their ecstasy they could see only a garden of flowers, some fresh and beautiful, others faded and worn. Nyina wa Jambo asked the girls to water the flowers they saw before them. The fresh flowers were the people who had turned to God, while the faded flowers were those who were absorbed in worldly things and had been worn down by the cares of the world. Mary warned them against materialism. 'You are distracted by the goods of this world,' Mary told Alphonsine. 'I have seen many of my children getting lost and I have come to show them the true way.'

Mary cared for the girls physically, too. Alphonsine had suffered from quinsy and an eye disease, and had lost her voice. Mary healed her of all these afflictions. It was as if she was strengthening her child for the future, but her preparation was not only physical. Another time, Alphonsine warned her classmates and teacher that she might appear dead but should not be buried. Then, with priests, nurses, nuns and a Red Cross worker looking on, she fell into a deep sleep. Her body became heavy and rigid, her hands frozen in a gesture of prayer. Over the next eighteen hours, Nyina wa Jambo guided Alphonsine on a journey through hell, purgatory and heaven.

Mary's most insistent message was a call to peace. 'Follow the Gospel of my son,' she said. 'Do not forget that God is more powerful than all the evil in the world . . . Respect the rights of man, because if you act contrary to those rights, your actions will fail and will come back against you.'

Alphonsine alone continued to see the apparitions for many years. On 28 November 1989, the seventh anniversary of the first visitation, Mary made a final appearance before her. This date has become the feast of Our Lady of Kibeho, a day on which Rwandans honour and remember Mary's apparitions.

During her last visit Mary said, 'I speak to those who hold power, and who represent the nation: save the people, instead of being their torturers. Don't rob the people; share with others. Be careful not to persecute, to muzzle those who want to denounce your errors.

'There is dissension, trouble, hatred all over the world,' she warned Alphonsine, imploring her to pray for the bishops of Rwanda, heads of state, and for the whole world. But why Rwanda, why this time? As always, time soon revealed greater levels of meaning to the Marian apparitions.

Rwanda, a small, landlocked country, is known as the African Switzerland for its scenic, hilly landscape. Unfortunately it has not always been a peaceful land. There were long-simmering tensions between the country's two ethnic communities, the Tutsis and the Hutus, and in 1994 they erupted into a horrifically violent civil war. Perhaps a million Tutsis and Hutus were killed. Among them was Marie-Claire. She was just thirty-three years old. In 1995, fighting broke out among the residents of a refugee camp at Kibeho. An estimated 4000 to 8000 people were murdered, some in the same school where Mary had appeared.

After the war, the survivors remembered Nyina wa Jambo and wondered. If enough people had listened to her message, perhaps all that destruction and pain could have been prevented.

The Catholic Church officially recognised the apparitions of the three girl visionaries as authentic in 2001. Rwandans prayed that the message of the apparitions would sustain their nation through its fragile peace. 'I hope that through Our Lady, Kibeho will become a centre for national reconciliation,' said Archbishop Augustin Misago, reflecting on the apparitions. At the same time he recognised that they were a gift for the whole world.

The twenty-fifth anniversary of the first apparition at Kibeho was celebrated with a special Mass. An estimated 10,000 pilgrims gathered in prayer at the shrine dedicated to Our Lady of Sorrows. As they reflected on Mary's apparitions, some of Nyina wa Jambo's simple words to Alphonsine seemed to sum up the meaning of her vists: 'I love you very much. If I came, it is because you needed it.'

We believe that you are amongst us, like a mother in the midst of her children, even though we do not see you with our bodily eyes.

You were gracious enough to appear miraculously in Kibeho, just when our world needed it most.

Teach us how to pray with sincerity and to love one another as Christ loved us, so that, just as you have requested, we may always be beautiful flowers diffusing their pleasant fragrance everywhere and upon everyone.

*And, when our pilgrimage on this earth comes to an end, may
we live eternally with you in the kingdom of heaven. Amen.*
—Prayer to Our Lady of Kibeho

A Garland of Roses

An ancient legend tells of a young monk in prayer. As
he recited each Hail Mary, it formed a delicate
rosebud, which Mary took from his lips. She then
weaved the precious flowers into a garland, and
placed them on her head.

It was the rosary, a prayer using beads and repetition of words to inspire contemplation. As the
Church spread and evolved, so did the devotion,
through Europe, Russia, Romania and Greece. It is a
prayer that brings peace, and one which Our Lady
has often called for in her apparitions, in Kibeho,
Akita and Fátima. Many miracles have been attributed to the rosary, from great victories in battle to
cures and conversions.

'Rosary' means a crown of roses, a spiritual
bouquet given to the Blessed Mother. But it is also a
prayer through which Mary gives her own spiritual
gifts to her people.

*My impression is that Our Lady wanted to give ordinary
people, who might not know how to pray, this simple method
of getting closer to God.*
—A reflection on the rosary by Sister Lucia,
one of the three visionaries of Fátima

The Rosary Dream

The bells awakened me—the same bells that were to signal the start of each segment of each day's itinerary. I was on a silent retreat in rural Ontario, a welcome break from my stress-filled life. Words were spoken only in prayer. Bells led us to prayers and then to the public rosary.

As the leader recited the prayers, he walked. We all followed in single file. He recited the first part, and we completed the prayer in unison. But to my horror, the other men began to race through the responses as though there was a prize for the first to finish.

At school I'd been taught to pray the rosary in a slow, reverent cadence. The idea was to meditate. How could that be done if the prayers were said hurriedly? My mind reeling, I went back to my room and lay down. Praying to Mary, I drifted off to sleep.

I found myself back on the retreat grounds, but I wasn't alone and I wasn't walking. I was about four feet above the ground, gliding at the pace of a stroll. Our Lady was beside me, walking with me as though we were the closest of friends.

She spoke to me as though she was sure I would understand her request. There was no audible conversation, but it was clearer than conversation. Mary made it known to me that she wished me to build a rosary—not to string one together but to sculpt one. She also wanted it in an environment that would encourage prayerful meditation on the mysteries of the rosary. As we 'walked', she 'spoke' very softly, explaining to the last detail the design and layout of the rosary I was to build. It would be a rosary with large beads; pilgrims would walk from one to the next, and this would slow their recitation to a proper cadence for meditation. 'Only then,' she said, 'will people learn the lessons of his life which are revealed through the recitation of the rosary.'

As she spoke, we were travelling the rosary's paths. I remember the tremendous feeling of peace that filled me. We were on about 100 acres of rolling hills, with beautiful trees, a running stream, and wildlife in abundance. The rosary wound through this natural landscape. Its beads were about a metre in diameter, each with a kneeling notch carved into its side, allowing pilgrims to stop and pray. A path went from one bead to the next, and the beads were linked together with a stainless-steel chain. They were cast in ceramic and glazed purple with a red flash like a tongue of fire. The circle of beads joined at a large fountain. In the centre of that fountain was a large sphere with a silhouette of Our Lady with Jesus.

Between the sets of ten Hail Mary beads were oval-shaped Our Father beads, wooden, screened gazebos in which pilgrims could sit on benches. A breathtaking wood and steel crucifix marked the beginning of the walk.

'Pilgrims who come here will be healed and enlightened,' Our Lady explained. 'When they return home, they will practise the holy rosary as they have never done before. Many souls will be brought to my blessed son.' Before parting, I asked where the rosary shrine should be built. 'You will know,' she said. Then I awoke.

I searched for a pen or pencil to sketch what I had seen, then I bolted out of my room. Was Our Lady still here? No, it was a dream. Or was it? Questions thundered through my mind. I searched for someone to talk to. I saw my friend John walking in the gardens of the retreat. 'I have something fantastic to tell you!' I shouted. Reluctantly breaking the silence, he said: 'Where have you been?' 'What do you mean?' I replied. 'We've been looking for you. Don't you realise that it's Sunday, two o'clock? Everyone's getting ready to go home.'

I had slept for over twenty-four hours.

I couldn't wait to get home and put it all down on paper before I forgot the details.

Within days I had finished a set of rough drawings and begun building a model. Over several months, I viewed the model from every angle. It rested on two ping-pong tables, and each tree, shrub, and bead was to scale.

Had this been just a dream or was it a religious encounter? Why was this project entrusted to me? I discussed the matter with trusted priests and friends. I decided to put the whole thing to the test of time. So I dismantled the model and put away the drawings.

Time passed, but the idea continued to pursue me. I studied Fine Arts. I am still continuing my search for the right place, and the right time, to make the rosary shrine a reality.

Many years have passed since the rosary dream began. The dream goes on and will be realised. My faith in God is boundless. Let his will be done.

—Ted, Manresa, Canada

Mary of Fátima
— Portugal —

As World War I ravaged Europe, the village of Fátima was not immune. Portugal was in chaos. Many Portuguese men were away fighting in France and Africa, and unstable governments rose and fell in the wake of the 1910 revolution.

According to legend, Fátima took its name from a Moorish princess, who in turn was named after the daughter of the Prophet Mohammed. In the 12th century, during the Islamic occupation of Portuguese territory, the princess was captured by Christians and converted to Catholicism.

Ten-year-old Lucia Abobora and her cousins, nine-year-old Francisco Marto and seven-year-old Jacinta Marto, lived with their extended family in a little hamlet less than a mile from Fátima. Like many children of their time, they were illiterate. Lucia had been working as a shepherdess since the age of seven in the sun-scorched fields around the town. Stunted oak trees and twisted olive groves dotted the countryside, in fields separated by crude stone walls.

Lucia was a strong, pious girl, blessed with an excellent memory. When she was seven, she had her first strange experience out in the fields. As she prayed the rosary with a group of shepherd children, a white, human shape seemed to move across the valley towards them, then vanished as their prayer concluded. Something similar happened on two other occasions, but the girls were dismissed as silly and the whole affair was soon forgotten.

Some time later her little cousins Francisco and Jacinta, after much pleading, were finally allowed to accompany Lucia as she went out shepherding.

Francisco's thoughtful and easygoing nature was in stark contrast to his little sister Jacinta's lively, sensitive personality. The quietly spoken Francisco would strive to resolve disputes; little Jacinta would shrink from them. They were alike only in appearance.

The three children passed the days singing, playing cards and chasing butterflies. Francisco would play his whistle while the girls danced. When they stopped for lunch they would pray an abridged version of the rosary, saying only the words Hail Mary and Our Father instead of the full prayers.

One summer morning near Cabeço, they were playing in the fields. A sudden burst of rain drove them from their games and their flocks to the shelter of a nearby cave encircled by an olive grove. They ate lunch and said a quick rosary, and when the weather improved they began to play a game with pebbles. A strong breeze swept by, and as they looked up, they saw a glowing figure moving towards them from across the valley.

Lucia later recalled the breathtaking apparition. 'We began to see, in the distance, above the trees that stretched to the east, a light whiter than snow in the form of a young man, quite transparent, and as brilliant as crystal in the rays of the sun. As he came near we were able to see his features. We were astonished and absorbed and we said nothing to one another.'

'Don't be afraid,' said the beautiful young man in a reassuring tone. 'I am the Angel of Peace. Pray with me.' With these words he knelt, his head to the ground, then taught them a simple prayer: *O my Jesus, forgive us our sins and save us from the fires of hell. And bring all souls to heaven, especially those in most need of thy mercy*. 'Pray thus,' he urged them, rising to his feet. 'The most holy hearts of Jesus and Mary will be touched by your prayer. They are ready to listen to you,' he added, then vanished.

Some twenty years later, Lucia wrote down her recollections of this profound moment. 'He left us in an atmosphere of the supernatural that was so intense we were for a long time unaware of our own existence. The presence of God was so powerful and intimate that even among ourselves we could not speak. On the next day, too, this same atmosphere held us bound, and it lessened and disappeared only gradually. None of us thought of talking about this apparition or any pledge of secrecy. Silence seemed to impose itself on us.

'His words sank so deeply into our minds that we never forgot them, and ever after we used to spend long periods on our knees repeating them, sometimes until we fell down exhausted.'

Their visitor later identified himself as the Angel of Portugal. He appeared twice more to the children, teaching them how to pray.

The children continued to follow his instructions for nearly eight months. It was May, 1917, and the three children were driving their sheep to pasture on the hilly land known as Cova da Iria. The war had been raging for three years now, and to the north, Russia was just months away from the Bolshevik revolution. For three innocent peasant children, it was just another day at work.

On the green slopes of the Cova, the children had finished their packed lunch and begun to pray their shortened rosary when they were startled by a flash of lightning in the clear blue sky. Fearing a storm, they prepared their flock for the journey home. As they headed towards the road, another lightning flash struck near a holm oak tree, and a few steps on, near another holm oak, they saw the figure that would change their lives forever: 'A lady dressed in white, shining brighter than the sun, giving out rays of clear and intense light, just like a crystal goblet full of pure water when the fiery sun passes through it.' The children stopped and stared, amazed. 'We were so near that we were in the light that encircled her, or which she radiated.'

'Please don't be afraid of me,' said the figure in a warm, loving voice.

Lucia was the first to respond. 'Where are you from?' she asked.

'I come from heaven.'

The woman's white mantle, edged with gold, fell right to her feet, and her soft white hands held a rosary that gleamed with beads like stars. The children were dumbfounded. Why would such an amazing woman choose to visit them?

She said that she planned to visit the children at the same hour, at the same place, on the thirteenth day of each month for the next six months. She promised to reveal her identity, and to grant them the greatest desires of their hearts.

Lucia was filled with excitement and started firing questions at the woman. 'And shall I go to heaven? And Jacinta? And Francisco?'

The lady assured the girls that they would go to heaven. 'Francisco, too, my dear,' she added, 'but he will first have many rosaries to say!'

Remembering some friends who had died, Lucia asked if they were in heaven. The woman answered all her questions patiently, then presented the three children with a challenge. 'Will you offer yourselves to God, and bear all the sufferings he sends you? In atonement for all the sins that offend him? And for the conversion of sinners?'

The children said yes.

The woman warned of great trials ahead but promised that the grace of God would strengthen them. Then she spread her arms, and an extraordinary light reached out and embraced the three children. Somehow they knew this was a light from God, and in sheer awe they fell to their knees.

The lady spoke of the war in Europe, but the children knew little of the world beyond their olive groves and pastures. 'Say the rosary every day to bring peace to the world and an end to the war,' the lady instructed them. Then she rose, moving slowly east until she disappeared. The light she emanated seemed to pull aside the sky like a veil, as if heaven opened for her.

Lucia made the two younger children promise to keep the incident a secret. But little Jacinta's excitement was uncontainable, and she told the story to the whole family. Jacinta's mother listened with calm indifference but her father, Ti, believed his daughter's tale. He knew his children were honest, and he had great faith in miracles.

Lucia's mother, Maria Rosa, wasn't impressed. To her mind the story was at best a fib, and at worst out-and-out blasphemy. She told Lucia to admit the story was made up, but Lucia refused. Her father was unmoved by what he considered 'the fancies of women', so Maria Rosa took her naughty child before the parish priest, Father Ferreira. Lucia stubbornly refused to take back her story.

The 13 June feast of St Anthony of Lisbon was approaching and Maria Rosa hoped the exciting day of fun and festivities in the village would distract her daughter from her fanciful stories. She was mistaken.

On 13 June, the three children dutifully turned up for their midday appointment with Mary. A small group of people had also gathered, curious to see what would happen.

With another flash of lightning, Mary appeared. But only the children could see her, and only the two girls could hear her. She told them to pray for those in need to be brought to heaven and to pray the rosary every day. She encouraged them to learn to read and write.

Lucia had more questions. 'Will you take us to heaven?' she asked.

'Yes,' the lady replied. 'I shall take Jacinta and Francisco soon, but you will remain a little longer, since Jesus wishes you to make me known and loved on earth. He wishes also for you to establish devotion in the world to my Immaculate Heart.'

This traditional belief held that the heart of Mary was an abundant source of pure love for God and for all people.

Lucia was concerned about her fate. 'Must I remain in the world alone?' she wondered sadly.

'Not alone, my child, and you must not be sad,' Mary assured her. 'I will be with you always, and my Immaculate Heart will be your comfort and the way which will lead you to God.'

Later, Lucia would recall the power of Mary's presence: 'The moment she said the last words, opening her hands, she transmitted to us, for the second time, the reflection of that intense light. In it we felt we were submerged in God.' Jacinta and Francisco seemed to be in that part of the light which was rising to heaven, and I in the part spreading over the earth. In front of the palm of Our Lady's right hand was a heart encircled with thorns which appeared to pierce it. We understood it was the Immaculate Heart of Mary . . .'

As Mary faded once again into the east, the three children were left to ponder her meaning. She had told them of a bleak future: an early death for the younger children and a lonely life for their cousin.

As for the bystanders, the most any of them had seen was a spark or flash, or a slight dimming of the sun. Others noticed a little grey cloud moving when the children said Mary moved. Only a few of them were convinced.

A month later, with a flash of light, Mary appeared as she had before. But this time she gave the children a three-fold message that would become known as the Three Secrets of Fátima, messages that were not recorded until Lucia wrote them down in 1941 at the request of a bishop.

The first secret was a brief but frightening vision of hell, the second a forewarning of the coming power of communist Russia. The Blessed Virgin begged for the consecration of Russia to her Immaculate Heart. It seemed odd that a country known for its great faith and long history of Christianity should need conversion. At the time of the apparition, Russia was not yet communist.

The third and most closely guarded secret was finally revealed by Pope John Paul II in 2000. It was a vision of an angel with a flaming sword, and clusters of mournful priests and religious, led by the Pope, climbing a steep mountain to the foot of a large cross. 'Before reaching there, the Holy Father passed through a big city half in ruins,' Lucia wrote. 'Half trembling, with halting step, afflicted with pain and sorrow . . . having reached the top of the mountain, on his knees at the foot of the big cross he was killed by a group of soldiers who fired bullets and arrows at him . . .'

This image was later interpreted as the 1981 assassination attempt on the Pope.

Lucia begged the lady to tell them who she was. She promised to reveal her identity in October, and to work a great miracle that would convince all doubters.

Meanwhile, everyone wanted to know the secrets. Family, friends, neighbours, Church and civil officials tried everything from coaxing to trickery to get the children to talk. Curious crowds surrounded their little Abóbora cottage, grasping at the three little children. 'In the hands of those people, we were like a ball in the hands of a little girl,' Lucia later wrote. 'Each one pulled us in his direction and asked his question, without ever giving us time to answer anybody.'

The local administrator was determined to prove that the children were lying. He took them to his home for questioning, then the town hall, and finally threw them in jail. Nothing would make them talk. They missed their next appointment with Mary.

The confused crowd at the Cova da Iria began praying the rosary at noon. A faint murmuring and rumble of thunder preceded the usual flash of light. A frail white cloud drifted low overhead, then floated up and blended into the sky. Red, yellow, blue, orange, brilliant colours seemed to reflect everywhere from no source in particular. It seemed that Mary had kept her appointment, though her children were missing.

The administrator bullied and browbeat the children, making all kinds of threats. They cried, they were frightened, but they would not betray the secrets. He finally released them on 15 August, the feast of the Assumption.

Joyfully back in their parents' arms, only one fear remained for the children. By missing their appointment, had they upset Mary? Would they ever see her again?

The answer came unexpectedly. A devout local woman, Maria Carriera, had erected a table adorned with flowers and an arch decorated with crosses and lamps at the site of the apparition. Pilgrims had left donations there, and, unsure what to do with the money, she approached Lucia for advice. 'God defend me!' Lucia cried, 'I don't want it either!' But she said she would ask Mary what to do with it when—and if—she next appeared.

That same morning, Lucia, Francisco and his brother John were out in the fields. They wandered and played and prayed, and by four in the afternoon they found themselves not far from the Cova da Iria.

All at once the atmosphere shifted. There was a sudden, deep sense of anticipation. Our Lady was coming. John ran to fetch Jacinta, who arrived in time to see the olive trees turn a distinctive silver. And there in the shimmering light the lady appeared.

'What do you want of me?' cried Lucia.

'Come again to the Cova da Iria on the thirteenth of next month, my child,' Mary replied gently, 'and continue to say the rosary every day. In the last month I will perform a miracle so that all may believe.'

'What are we to do with the offerings of money that people leave at the Cova da Iria?' asked Lucia.

'I want you to have two pedestals made, for the money is for the feast of Our Lady of the Rosary. I want you and Jacinta to carry one of them with two other girls dressed in white. Let Francisco, with three boys helping him, carry the other one. What is left over will help towards the support of the chapel that is to be built here.'

Lucia then asked for the cure of some sick people.

'Some I will cure during the year,' Mary promised. And she again begged them to pray and sacrifice for others.

On 13 September, Lucia, Francesco and Jacinta gathered at the Cova da Iria once again, but this time some 30,000 eager pilgrims flooded the roads and fields. 'All wanted to see and talk with us,' Lucia later wrote. 'Many of them, even gentlemen and noblemen, broke through the press and knelt before us, asking us to present their necessities to Our Lady.'

At the stroke of midday, a luminous globe appeared in the sky, gliding from east to west. An awed hush fell over the crowd. People began pointing to the sky. Mary was bathed in a glorious white light, 'more beautiful than the most brilliant light of the sun,' Francisco recalled. 'More beautiful than anyone I have ever seen.'

Lucia humbly asked her usual question. 'What do you want of me?'

The Blessed Mother repeated her desire to hear her children pray the rosary. 'Say it every day, that the war may end,' she implored.

Mary advised the children about the importance of prayer and penance. Lucia asked her about some of the many requests she had received. Mary gently promised to fulfil some, then repeated, 'In October I will perform a miracle so that all may believe.'

The night before the final apparition, there was a bad storm. Pilgrims of all ages and backgrounds struggled in darkness through mud, rain and icy gales, on foot, on animals, in carts and in cars, to the Cova da Iria. Journalist Avelino de Almeida described the scene. 'Nearly all, men and women, have bare feet, the women carrying their footgear in bags on their heads, the men leaning on great staves and carefully grasping umbrellas. One would say they were all oblivious to what was going on about them, with a great lack of interest in the journey and in other travellers, as if lost in a dream, reciting their rosary in a sad rhythmic chant. A woman says the first part of the Hail Mary; her companions in chorus say the second part of the prayer. With sure and rhythmical steps they tread the dusty road which runs between the pine woods and the olive groves, so that they may arrive before night at the place of the apparition, where, under the serene and cold light of the stars, they hope they can sleep.'

Next morning, as the rain continued to fall, the children pushed their way past the crowds of waiting pilgrims sheltering under black umbrellas. Midday came and went. Lucia called to the crowd to take down their umbrellas. They obeyed, but still nothing happened. The crowd began to murmur disapprovingly. Then Lucia's face brightened. 'Jacinta, kneel down, for now I see Our Lady there!' she called. 'I can see the flash!'

The children fell to their knees in the mud. Lucia asked her question for the final time. 'What do you want of me?'

'I want a chapel built here in my honour,' Mary replied. 'I want you to continue saying the rosary every day. The war will end soon, and the soldiers will return to their homes.'

'I have many things to ask you,' cried Lucia, trying desperately to remember all the prayer requests people had made.

'Some I shall grant, and others I must deny,' said Mary gently. 'People must amend their lives and ask pardon for their sins. They must not offend Our Lord any more, for he is already too much offended!' Then, as her arms opened in a wide embrace, white light blazed out, more brilliant than the sun. The crowd saw no one, but watched as the clouds rolled back like great curtains and the sun shone from a blue sky.

'Look at the sun!' cried Lucia. She would never remember saying those words. She was in ecstasy. Before her eyes three scenes unfolded. Mary appeared beside Joseph, who held the infant Jesus in his arms. 'Saint Joseph is going to bless us!' cried Lucia, as he raised his hand. Joseph and the infant Jesus blessed the pilgrims three times.

In the second scene, viewed only by Lucia, Mary was in an agony of grief, watching Jesus take his final steps on the path to his crucifixion. Only the upper part of his body was visible as he looked at the assembled crowd of pilgrims and blessed them.

In the third vision, Mary appeared crowned as the Queen of Heaven, with her infant son on her lap.

As the children took in the visions, the crowds were distracted by other incredible sights. The sun began to shine brighter than ever. Remarkably, everyone could gaze on it unharmed. Then, as if in joy, the sun began to dance. It whirled like a gigantic catherine-wheel, stopping and starting, then released huge crimson flames that reflected all the colours of the rainbow. Everything in sight took on green, blue, violet, orange hues. Then all at once, the sun shuddered and seemed to zigzag down towards the astonished crowd.

People cried out and fell to their knees in prayer. It seemed that the end of the world was coming. After ten minutes the sun retreated, zigzagging back to its place in the sky, a familiar midday sun.

Recovering their senses, people began to shout. 'Miracle! Miracle! Blessed be God! Blessed be Our Lady!'

Laughing, weeping, tears streaming down their faces, they prayed and cried out with joy. People witnessed the miracle of the sun from many kilometres away. Some claimed they had seen what the children saw, while others said they saw the smiling face of Mary in the sky. No matter what they saw, everyone walked away from the Cova da Iria knowing they had seen something holy.

Finally convinced about the apparitions, the children's parents agreed to send the girls to school to learn to read and write as Mary had requested. Francisco, sure that he would die young, spent his days in prayer, wandering in the countryside or returning to the places where he had seen Mary. When he wasn't in prayer, he would perform acts of kindness for less fortunate neighbours, rounding up the sheep of an elderly lady who lived nearby, or praying for anyone who requested it.

In October 1918, as World War I was coming to an end, an influenza epidemic broke out, and Francisco's entire family was stricken. Francisco died in April 1919 of bronchial pneumonia. Not long after, Jacinta fell ill and was taken to hospital. After an operation she only seemed to get worse, but was comforted by visions of Mary by her bedside. She died in 1920.

In a few months Lucia had lost the only two people who understood what she had seen and shared her great secrets. When she was just fourteen, she entered the convent of the Sisters of Saint Dorothy at Vilar. From age eighteen to twenty-two, the Blessed Virgin appeared to Lucia three more times, encouraging her to pray. She spoke of how much she wanted Russia to be consecrated to her, repeating one of the secrets she had told the children in July 1917. Lucia followed Mary's promptings and joined the Carmelite sisters, an enclosed order devoted to prayer and contemplation. She died in 2005 at the age of ninety-seven. The following year, her remains were taken to the Shrine of Fátima, where they joined the remains of her two cousins.

The Chapel of Apparitions at the Cova da Iria today has a simple marble pillar bearing a statue of Our Lady of Fátima on the exact spot where she appeared. The holm oak tree where the children waited for Mary still stands nearby. A fragment of the Berlin Wall is also there, displayed in a monument to the fall of Soviet communism which Mary prophesied.

Our Lady of Fátima, cure the sick who confide in you.
Our Lady of Fátima, console the sorrowful who trust in you.
Our Lady of Fátima, obtain peace for the world.
—PART OF PRAYER TO OUR LADY OF FÁTIMA, CARDINAL
PATRIARCH, LISBON, 31 NOVEMBER, 1938

Memories of a Dancing Sun

I was only nine years old at this time, and I went to the local village school. At about midday we were surprised by the shouts and cries of some men and women who were passing in the street in front of the school. The teacher, a good, pious woman, though nervous and impressionable, was the first to run into the road, with the children after her.

Outside, the people were shouting and weeping and pointing to the sun, ignoring the agitated questions of the schoolmistress. It was the great miracle, which one could see quite distinctly from the top of the hill where my village was situated—the miracle of the sun, accompanied by all its extraordinary phenomena.

I feel incapable of describing what I saw and felt. I looked fixedly at the sun, which seemed pale and did not hurt the eyes. Looking like a ball of snow revolving on itself, it suddenly seemed to come down in a zigzag, menacing the earth. Terrified, I ran and hid myself among the people, who were weeping and expecting the end of the world at any moment.

Near us was an unbeliever who had spent the morning mocking the simpletons who had gone off to Fátima just to see an ordinary girl. He now seemed to be paralysed, his eyes fixed on the sun. Afterwards he trembled from head to foot and, lifting up his arms, fell on his knees in the mud, crying out to Our Lady . . .

We all ran to the two chapels in the village, which were soon filled to overflowing. During those long moments of the solar prodigy, objects around us turned all the colours of the rainbow. We saw ourselves blue, yellow, red, etc. All these strange phenomena increased the fears of the people. After about ten minutes the sun, now dull and pallid, returned to its place. When the people realised that the danger was over, there was an explosion of joy, and everyone joined in thanksgiving and praise to Our Lady.

—Father Ignacio Lorenço, witness of the miracle from Alburitel, sixteen kilometres away

A Gift from the Queen of Carmel

In the 13th century Mount Carmel was a centre for prayer and contemplation. People had sheltered in its majestic caves for centuries. Some formed communities, and became known as Carmelites, a group dedicated to Mary. With the Crusades came violent Saracen invasions and in 1235 the Carmelites fled. Some Crusaders, seeking a more peaceful way of life, joined them. As they spread all over the world in their inner search for God, they encountered countries and people far removed from their desert homes.

Simon Stock was born in a castle at Harford in England. The child of a great English family, he left home at age twelve to live in the hollow trunk of an oak tree. He lived on water, herbs, roots and wild apples in a life of solitude and prayer. In his struggles he would turn to Mary for consolation.

Simon left the forests and joined the Carmelite order, and with his help it spread through Cambridge,

Oxford, Paris and Bologna. But by 1251, Simon was nearly seventy, and community life was exhausting. He retreated to his cell to pray. Mary appeared, her arms outstretched and holding a circular piece of cloth to the elderly man. 'This shall be the privilege for you and for all the Carmelites,' she said, 'that anyone dying in this habit shall be saved.'

Simon obediently distributed copies of this cloth to his Carmelite brothers, and it became known as the scapular. And so began a great devotion which spread all over the world. Kings and common-ers lived and died wearing the scapular, hidden beneath their clothes. It is usually in the form of a pure wool cloth worn over the shoulders, adorned with small images of Mary embroidered in the fabric. It is a reassurance of Mary's protection, and a promise to live a life of faith and love. Mary appeared with the scapular at Fátima, prompting many to put on the scapular once again.

Mother of Hope
— Poland —

On the day Karol Josef Wojtyla was born, Poland was celebrating. It had just been recognised as an independent nation in the Treaty of Versailles. But it was still a nation in conflict, still in the throes of its post–World War I struggle against Soviet Russia. A few months later, the miracle of the Vistula, attributed to Our Lady of Czestochowa, would grant the Poles another great victory. In this turbulent world, Mary was to play an extraordinary role in young Karol's life.

It was a difficult life for Karol. His mother died when he was only eight years old. His loving and devoted father did his best to raise him alone, but he too passed away, when Karol was twenty. During the Nazi occupation many of his family and friends perished. When the Soviets occupied the country, Karol was forced to undertake his training as a priest in an underground seminary. Even though his beloved Church was persecuted, Mary always seemed to keep him safe. He repaid her care with deep devotion, reading many books about her, especially those of the Carmelite saints. When he was made a bishop, he took as his coat of arms the letter M, for Mary, and as his motto *Totus tuus*, I am all yours.

In 1978, Karol made history when he was elected as the first non-Italian Pope in over 450 years. Taking the name Pope John Paul II, he immediately began to challenge convention. Rejecting all recommendations, he retained his simple 'M' coat of arms and his *Totus tuus* motto.

He took up his new responsibilities with enthusiasm and dedication, and people everywhere loved this smiling, charismatic Pope. He made a point of reaching out to them, travelling the world seeking unity and peace, and praying before the many shrines of his beloved Mary. He became known as the Pilgrim Pope, as he travelled more than any of his predecessors.

On 13 May 1981, Pope John Paul II was greeting crowds at St Peter's in Rome when the sound of shots rang out. As pigeons flew into the air, horrified onlookers saw that the Pope had been shot.

As an ambulance sped him to hospital, Pope John Paul II murmured his prayers. His blood pressure dropped, his heart rate fell, and as his blood drained from his body, the Pope lost consciousness. Five hours of surgery ensued, in an attempt to repair the damage. Two American pilgrims were also wounded. It was the anniversary of Mary's first apparition at Fátima.

Meanwhile, some Polish pilgrims had brought a copy of Our Lady of Czestochowa to the Vatican. They placed it in the empty chair where the Pope was supposed to sit. When a gust of wind blew it over, there on the back was the recently written inscription, 'May Our Lady protect the Holy Father from evil'.

The loyal crowd remained in St Peter's Square, praying the rosary continuously. Then, after midnight, news came that the Pope's surgery had been a success, and that his condition was satisfactory.

Mehmet Ali Agca, the professional assassin who fired his pistol at close range, had missed the Pope's major arteries, spinal column and every major nerve cluster by mere inches. One bullet fell to the floor of the Pope's vehicle, where it was later found. Had it too hit its target, Pope John Paul II might have bled to death before he reached the ambulance.

On 17 May the recovering Pope pre-recorded his regular Sunday midday message to pilgrims, in which he empathised with his fellow victims. 'I pray for that brother of ours who shot me,' he added, 'and whom I have sincerely pardoned. United with Christ, priest and victim, I offer my sufferings for the Church and for the world. To you, Mary, I repeat: *Totus tuus ego sum*.' I am all yours.

During his convalescence, the Pope asked for all Vatican documents on Fátima and the apparitions of Mary.

In hospital, he read the letter from Sister Lucia, the last surviving Fátima visionary, describing the third secret of Fátima. 'The Holy Father will have much to suffer,' Mary had declared. In the prophetic vision the children saw a man in white robes, whom they assumed to be the Pope, 'afflicted with pain and sorrow' and suffering under a hail of bullets and arrows.

The Pope resolved to properly fulfil Mary's request to consecrate Russia to her Immaculate Heart. The date of the 1984 consecration was the shared anniversary of the attempt on his life and Mary's first appearance in Fátima. Pope John Paul II asked for a statue of Our Lady of Fátima to be taken to a small church on the border of Poland and the Soviet Union, positioned with its gaze towards Russia.

The Pope gave the bullet found in his vehicle to the Bishop of Fátima, who placed it in the crown of the statue of Our Lady of Fátima, where it remains to this day. 'It was a mother's hand that guided the bullet's path,' the Pope later said. 'My mother forever, and especially on May 13, 1981, when I felt your helpful presence at my side.'

In 1983, Pope John Paul II went to visit his would-be murderer in jail. Sitting together on black plastic chairs, the two men spoke for some time. As a professional hitman, Agca was still confused about what had gone wrong in his plans. 'Why didn't you die? I know that my aim was true, and I know that the bullet was very powerful and mortal . . . so why didn't you die?' he asked the Pope.

'One hand fired the shot,' the Pope replied simply. 'Another hand guided it.' He had no doubt that that hand was Mary's.

While in prison, Agca had read about Fátima and the prophecy of the assassination attempt, and he had come to believe that the 'Goddess of Fátima' had protected the Pope and imprisoned him. Now he feared Mary's vengeance. Pope John Paul II gently explained that Mary loved everyone, so he had nothing to be concerned about.

The Pope later visited Fátima twice to give thanks for his life. 'At the very moment I fell,' he said, 'I had this vivid presentiment that I should be saved.'

Visiting Fátima again on the tenth anniversary of the attempt on his life, he said, 'I consider this decade to be a gift, given to me in a special way by Divine Providence,' then knelt in silent prayer before the statue whose crown contained a bullet from Agca's gun. There in Fátima, he prayed to the maternal figure who had guided and protected him all his life.

Could I forget that the event in St Peter's Square took place on the day and at the hour when the first appearance of the Mother of Christ to the poor little peasants has been remembered for over sixty years at Fátima, Portugal? For in everything that happened to me on that very day, I felt that extraordinary motherly protection and care, which turned out to be stronger than the deadly bullet.

—POPE JOHN PAUL II, *MEMORY AND IDENTITY*, 2005

The Weeping Statue of Akita
— Japan —

T he ancient city of Akita is surrounded by green mountains in the east and the Sea of Japan to the west. At nearby Yuzawadai, nestled beside the clear waters of Tazawa Lake, the deepest in Japan, a group of women live in a community of prayer and devotion known as the Institute of the Handmaids of the Eucharist.

Agnes Katsuko Sasagawa entered this convent at the age of forty-two. After converting from Buddhism, she had developed a deep love of Mary. But the new lifestyle was difficult for her, especially as she was almost completely deaf. Over the years Agnes had had around twenty operations. While she could speak, she could understand others only through lip reading.

She had been 'Sister' Agnes for barely a month when she witnessed the first of many strange events.

One June evening, Sister Agnes was praying in the chapel when her eyes were drawn to a brilliant light shining from the tabernacle on the altar, where the eucharist was kept. A fine mist, like smoke, seemed to drift around the altar. At one point she was amazed to see 'a multitude of beings similar to angels, who surrounded the altar in adoration before the Host'. Sister Agnes asked the other nuns if they'd noticed anything unusual, but they said no. Sister Agnes continued to witness these strange manifestations on several occasions.

A lovely visitor also began appearing to Sister Agnes, a figure with 'a round face, an expression of sweetness . . . a person covered with a shining whiteness like snow'. She was sure it was none other than her guardian angel, and they regularly talked and prayed together.

On one visit the angel asked her to pray the Fátima prayer as she prayed the rosary. Japan in 1973 was not a place or time that knew much, if anything, of Fátima, let alone the prayers three Portuguese shepherd children learned in apparitions over fifty years earlier. Sister Agnes listened obediently and did her best to learn the words the angel taught her: *O my Jesus, forgive us our sins, and save us from the fires of hell. Lead all souls to heaven, especially those in most need of thy mercy. Amen.* The other sisters in Sr Agnes' community soon learned this prayer, and they taught it to the people who visited them.

About two weeks after she first saw the light coming from the tabernacle, Sister Agnes discovered a cross-shaped cut on the palm of her left hand. A week later, blood started to flow from it. Sometimes she barely noticed the wound. At other times she would suffer greatly from the pain. The day after the bleeding began, the angel went with her into the chapel, then vanished. Not knowing what else to do, Sister Agnes turned to the statue of Mary. 'I suddenly felt that the wooden statue came to life and was about to speak to me,' she recalled. 'She was bathed in a brilliant light . . . and at the same moment a voice of indescribable beauty struck my totally deaf ears.'

'Your deafness will be healed,' promised the sweet, gentle voice. 'Be patient.'

Mary began to pray with her. Then the angel reappeared, and the three prayed in unison. Sister Agnes listened to their celestial voices, and felt she was in heaven.

The next morning, when the sisters gathered for prayer, they found blood coming from the statue's hand—from a wound identical to the one on Sister Agnes' hand. On the next three Fridays, the statue and Sister Agnes bled simultaneously. The angel promised that Sister Agnes' bleeding would stop on

27 July, the feast of the Immaculate Heart of Mary, and it did, never to return.

The statue continued to bleed for another two months. 'It seemed to be truly cut into flesh,' wrote one of the sisters. 'The edge of the cross had the aspect of human flesh, and one even saw the grain of the skin like a fingerprint. I said to myself at that moment that the wound was real.'

When the statue's bleeding stopped, all the nuns watched as a bright light shone from the wooden form. The statue began to glisten with beads of moisture that looked like perspiration. A sweet perfume arose from it, and within a moment Sister Agnes' guardian angel was by her side, explaining that Mary was sad. 'Dry the perspiration,' the angel said. The sisters complied. From that moment, the statue's light began gradually to fade.

A few days later, Mary spoke to Sister Agnes again, emphasising the importance of obedience, and of prayer. 'Let each one endeavour, according to capacity and position, to offer herself entirely to the Lord,' she said. She spoke for the last time on the anniversary of the miracle of the sun at Fátima, in October 1973. 'Each day recite the prayers of the rosary. With the rosary pray for the Pope, the bishops and the priests. Those who place their confidence in me will be saved.'

Life became relatively normal again. Then, towards the end of May 1974, the sisters began to observe a curious change in the statue's appearance. Mary's clothes and hair remained the same, but the face, hands and feet turned a darker, reddish-brown hue.

The statue was the first Christian carving by Buddhist sculptor Saburo Wakasa. 'I sculpted the whole statue of Mary, the globe, and the cross from the same piece of wood, so there are no joints,' he said. The wood he used was hard and dry.

In January 1975, the statue began to weep. It wept three times on that first day. The local bishop and a number of visitors on retreat also witnessed the phenomenon. Sister Agnes discussed the matter with Bishop John Ito. He asked Professor Sagisaka, MD, a non-Christian specialist in forensic medicine to examine the residues of blood, sweat and tears taken from the statue. He was careful not to say where his samples came from.

The specialist found that the blood, sweat and tears were all human. The blood was type B, while the sweat and tears were type AB.

Sister Agnes' blood was also group B. At first there were concerns about trickery or self-deception, but a formal commission of inquiry found no evidence of it. Something supernatural had happened.

On 8 December 1979, the feast of the Immaculate Conception of Mary, a TV crew filmed the statue weeping. The images were broadcast on national television. The sculptor was asked many questions about his statue of Mary. He could tell people everything about what it was made from, and how it was carved, but he could not explain what was happening to it. 'It is a mystery,' was all he could say.

On 15 September 1981, the feast of Our Lady of Sorrows, the statue of Mary wept for the last time. Two weeks later, Sister Agnes' angel appeared to her with a large Bible bathed in light. It was open at Genesis 3:15. The angel told her that the passage explained Mary's tears. 'Sin came into the world by a woman [Eve] and it is also by a woman that salvation came to the world [Mary].'

Mary had wept 101 times in all, and between ten and sixty-five people had witnessed each weeping. Some were non-Christians, including the Buddhist mayor.

There were miracles of healing, too. In 1981, while praying before the statue of Mary, a Korean pilgrim was healed of terminal brain cancer. Then in 1982, Sister Agnes' hearing (which she had lost again in 1975) suddenly returned.

Bishop Ito was very supportive of Sister Agnes. 'She is a woman sound in spirit, frank and without problems,' he wrote.

'She has always impressed me as a balanced person. Consequently the messages she says that she has received did not appear to me to be in any way the result of imagination or hallucination.' He also noted the similarities between Mary's presence in Akita and in Fátima. 'The message of Akita is the message of Fátima,' he once said, and the Vatican supported his words with its approval of the events.

Sister Agnes continues to live an unremarkable life. She has moved out of the community house, but is still a member of the Seitai Hoshikai Handmaids of the Eucharist Community. Her time as a messenger of the miraculous is over, and she is content to live with the memories of her angel and of Mary.

A beautiful Japanese garden was built in the grounds of the convent of the Handmaids of the Eucharist, complete with a statue of Mary and tranquil waterways. Here, pilgrims still come to pray and contemplate the great graces Mary has visited upon Akita.

Most Holy Mother of God, never let me be separated from thy divine son. Please defend and protect me as thy special child.
—From the prayer of the Handmaids of the Eucharist

Mary of Dong Lu
— China —

In 1900, Dong Lu was a tiny, poor village in northern China, known by many as 'the place of beggars'. It was indistinguishable from many other villages in China at the time, except that it was home to around a thousand Christians. As the Boxer Rebellion swept the nation, this village became the target of 10,000 angry soldiers who were determined to stamp out any signs of westernisation, including Christianity.

On a dark day in April, as the soldiers attacked, a beautiful lady robed in white appeared in the heavens. She was bathed in a serene light. The soldiers fired into the sky, but no bullet found its target. Instead, the apparition shone as brightly as ever. Before the soldiers could recover from their shock, a fiery horseman also appeared. This lone warrior, believed to be Saint Michael the Archangel, descended on the soldiers and drove them out of Dong Lu. Ten thousand men defeated by a single angel on a blazing horse. But where had the heavenly lady and her defender come from? Father Wu, the local Chinese priest, offered one possible explanation. In his fear and desperation, he said, he had done the only thing he could think of. He had prayed to Mary.

The grateful villagers built a church in honor of the beautiful Virgin who had come to their aid. Father Wu obtained a painting of the emperor's mother dressed in imperial robes, and commissioned an artist to paint Mary and the infant Jesus in the style of the empress's portrait. The final painting was reverently placed in the church of Dong Lu, where grateful devotees came to pray.

In 1924, Our Lady of Dong Lu was officially recognised as Our Lady of China, and 6 May was chosen as her special day.

When the communists took over in China, they outlawed religion. In 1951 the church was destroyed along with the image of Our Lady of China. Only a modest shrine to Our Lady of Dong Lu remained in Hubei.

In May 1995, Catholics from all over China travelled to the Dong Lu shrine to celebrate the feast of Our Lady Help of Christians. Despite road blocks and other attempts to stop the pilgrimage, an estimated 30,000 pilgrims gathered on the 'hill of the blessed mother'.

During the ceremonies the pilgrims, along with four bishops and nearly 100 priests, witnessed a miracle. The sun seemed to spin from left to right and emit rays of light of varying colours. Our Lady of China appeared in the sky once again, holding the infant Jesus. Bathed in light, Mary had returned to give comfort to the oppressed, just as she had almost a century before.

The government in Beijing swiftly banned pilgrims from the Dong Lu shrine, and the following year it was destroyed. But the risk of imprisonment or worse has not stopped people from making the trip to the site. And many expatriates continue to keep alive the memory of Our Lady of Dong Lu.

Hail, Holy Mary, mother of Our Lord Jesus Christ, mother of all nations and all people. You are the special heavenly mother of the Chinese people. Teach us your way of total obedience to God's will. Help us to live our lives true to our faith. Fill our hearts with burning love for God and each other . . . Our Lady of China, mother of Jesus, hear our petitions and pray for us. Amen.

—Daisy Y. Y. Lin

Mary of La Vang
— Vietnam —

During the 18th century, Vietnam was in turmoil. The Trinh and Nguyen families struggled for control of the land. Peasant uprisings and violent clashes broke out everywhere.

The ruler, King Canh Thinh, feared that Catholics were helping his rival, so he began to oppress Christians. In 1798 he ordered all Catholic churches and seminaries to be destroyed. Catholics could only watch in horror as their holy places were desecrated. It was the beginning of a persecution that would last almost 100 years. Their only consolation in these years was Our Lady of La Vang.

Various legends surround her strange name. La Vang may derive from the name for the deep forests in central Vietnam, a type of fern, or the Vietnamese word for crying out, as many people did under this oppressive rule.

Our Lady of La Vang first appeared in 1798, when the great trial of Vietnamese Catholics was just beginning. Many escaped from the village of Quang Tri to seek shelter in the high mountain forests of La Vang, near the ancient capital Hue, but they were unprepared for the many hazards of life on the run. They battled freezing temperatures, sickness, animal attacks and starvation. They would huddle together at night to seek consolation in prayer.

It was on one of these dark evenings that Mary first appeared. A group of weary refugees was sitting on the damp grass near a huge banyan tree, praying. The calm night sky was suddenly brightened by the appearance of a beautiful woman in a long cape. In her arms was a baby boy. She was wearing a traditional Vietnamese dress, an *ao dai*, with a simple crown. The entire apparition was encircled in a great but gentle light. Two angels escorted Mary, who consoled the frightened people and offered some advice. By boiling the leaves of the surrounding plants and trees, they could make medicines to treat their illnesses, she said. She promised to be by their side through their trials, and to answer the prayers of all who gathered at that place to implore her assistance.

When the vision faded, the people were filled with hope and joy. They built a humble chapel with leaves and rice straw. As word of the apparition spread, people from far and wide made the perilous pilgrimage to this tiny, isolated chapel in the jungle. What began as a simple act of thanks and devotion became an annual procession.

Many Vietnamese Catholics were martyred. Thirty people were seized as they emerged from hiding places in the forest and burned alive. At their request, they died on the site of the chapel. The chapel itself seemed to be strangely protected. The government soldiers who enforced the persecutions had heard of the miraculous deeds at La Vang and never attempted to harm the building, perhaps fearing what might happen to them. When a fire broke out, the wooden altar and the candle-holders amazingly survived.

In 1802, the people emerged from the jungles of La Vang and returned to the villages with many grateful stories of Mary's loving care. For twenty years they lived in peace, visiting and maintaining the chapel in the forest. But then a new wave of anti-Catholic hostility led to the brutal deaths of 100,000 Vietnamese men, women and children.

In 1886, the persecution ended. The bishop ordered a new brick church to be built in honour of Our Lady of La Vang, who had comforted and consoled so many. Limited funding and the isolated location made the building a difficult task. It took fifteen years to finish. When it was finally completed, in 1901, over 12,000 people gathered for the two-day celebration. Eight years later, a larger church was opened, and La Vang was pronounced Mary's devotional centre in Vietnam. It remained a powerful place of worship until it was destroyed during the Vietnam War.

Everyone knew that the shrine of La Vang was special. According to one story, the ailing emperor of Vietnam was healed after he sent one of his ministers to pray at La Vang.

Five years after the country's reunification in 1975, all the bishops of Vietnam gathered in Hanoi, solemnly acknowledging their recognition of La Vang as Vietnam's national shrine to Mary. Together they sang the *Salve Regina* (Hail, Queen of Heaven) on their knees in a touching display of solidarity and faith.

Devotion to Our Lady of La Vang has spread throughout the world. In Louisville, Kentucky, there is a sanctuary in her honour, complete with statues, walkways and benches for pilgrims. In Vietnam, good works are still carried out in her name. Our Lady of La Vang first came to her people when they had nothing, not even a chapel. She continues to care for her people all over the world.

Blessed Lady of La Vang, be my mother and comfort me, especially in times of trial and unhappiness. Enter my heart and stay with me wherever I may go. Grant that one day, through you, I may find rest and peace in my Father's house.
—ANN BALL, PRAYER TO OUR LADY OF LA VANG

Our Lady's Protection

La Vang is where many Vietnamese people come to pray almost every day, especially people from the area, in the middle of Vietnam. Our ancestors from Tri Buu village were martyred because they were Catholic. Some escaped from the village by hiding in the mountain forests, to avoid the armies of the king. Their sanctuary, La Vang, is ten kilometres west of the village. At that time they were hungry, ill, lonely and scared. Mary appeared to care for and encourage them. She told the people to pick the nearby leaves, which the locals called la vang. *She told them how to eat the leaves, so the sick would be cured.*

Visitors to Our Lady's shrine in Quang Tri City can still see a lot of these la vang *leaves for sale around the shrine.*

My brothers and sisters and I were born near the shrine of Our

Lady of La Vang. We grew up at La Vang, and lived there for nearly twenty years. We left in 1975, but we kept praying to Our Lady.

When I was a little boy, I used to go with my parents to visit Our Lady of La Vang. Every month we'd make the pilgrimage on foot, and many people went there to do the same. We would cross the hills, surrounded by lush bushes all around. It was so thick it was like walking through a leafy green tunnel. Looking up, we would see the sunshine glinting through the leaves, but not the sun. La Vang in the 19th century was a mountainous, wild region, with lots of monkeys, tigers, birds, elephants, snakes . . . It was a dangerous place, and only the poor people went there to chop wood to sell for a living. That's why those early Christians went hiding there, to survive. When I was a small child in the late 1950s, early 1960s, it still felt much the same.

I can still remember what I saw as a young boy—hundreds of stone cards, with carved words: 'Thanks be to Mary La Vang,' all around the stone base of the Mary statue. They had been left by the many people who went there, who prayed and received graces from God through Mary.

The relationship between Our Lady of La Vang and my family has been very close. Every day we prayed, and twice on Sundays. The whole family would say the rosary together. Of course Mum and Dad always led the prayer, to motivate all the children to pray.

Our Lady of La Vang always answered our prayers, especially my parents' prayers to escape from Vietnam. We left in 1982. Before we began the trip our whole family went to visit Our Lady of La Vang. We prayed, and put our life in Mary's hands. We left home early in the morning and escaped by boat at nightfall. One hundred and thirty people were crammed into the tiny boat, only fifteen metres by five metres.

We sat on top of each other. It was a horrible scene. Starting from the small river near Vung Tau, we headed for the South China Sea. On the second day of the trip, the engine broke down, and our boat was left floating in the sea for five days! We had lost all sense of direction. When the first child died, we prayed and buried her in the ocean with a blanket.

Two-thirds of the people starting losing consciousness from lack of water and food. I prepared myself for death, too. The water under and around our boat was filled with big, dark-blue fish . . . it was terrifying! On the seventh night, we saw a vague light far away in the deep night sky. By early morning, our boat was floating beside a big petrol tanker, about 500 metres away. The crew saw us and rescued us from a horrible fate. Thanks to God and Mary!

Now I'm getting older, and I have my own family with three children. Day by day I realise more and more how much we really did receive from Our Lady, and how many graces we receive from God, no matter where we are or what we do. Escaping from South Vietnam was a great event for me. What a wonderful life I've had, with my trust in God and Mary's blessing! I am always very pleased to talk about God and Mary. I hope my story helps people to love Mary more.

—Minh Le, *Western Australia*

Mother of the Faithful
— China —

In 1952 Ignatius Kung Pin-mei, a Chinese bishop, declared a Year of Mary in Shanghai and sent a statue of Our Lady of Fátima on a tour of the city's beleaguered churches. At Christ the King Church, where a mass arrest of priests had occurred a month before, Bishop Kung led the rosary in full view of hundreds of armed police. Bishop Kung then prayed: 'Holy Mother, we do not ask you for a miracle. We do not beg you to stop the persecutions. But we beg you to support us who are very weak.'

Three years later, Bishop Kung, with some 200 priests and church leaders, was arrested. He was put in front of a microphone before a huge crowd and told to confess his crimes. He shouted 'Long live Christ the King! Long live the Pope!' and the crowd joined in. When questioned by the chief prosecutor, he said 'You can cut off my head, but you can never take away my faith.' He was given his sentence: life imprisonment.

Bishop Kung spent the next thirty years in jail, mostly in solitary confinement. He had no letters or visits, no Bible, no religious objects.

But on tiny pieces of thin rice paper, he managed to write. These fragile testaments of faith, hidden from the prison guards, miraculously survived the repeated searches of his cell. They were smuggled out of China, and first revealed at his funeral. 'Our Lady is indeed the mother of our salvation,' he wrote. Pressed to renounce his faith, he stoically refused. He was finally released from prison at the age of eighty-six.

Bishop Kung said he had consecrated his three dioceses—Shanghai, Nanking and Soochou—to Mary's Immaculate Heart while he was in jail. 'I am confident that in her own time, Our Lady of Fátima will save China just as she has saved Russia and Eastern Europe from religious persecution,' he said. 'Yes, Chinese Roman Catholics are very familiar with Our Lady of Fátima and her promises. There has always been a strong devotion to the rosary in China.'

When Bishop Kung finally travelled to Rome for a private audience with Pope John Paul II, he learned that he had been elevated to Cardinal years before during his long imprisonment. Even though he was frail and wheelchair bound, the new cardinal threw aside his cane and feebly walked up the steps to kneel respectfully before the Pope. Visibly touched, Pope John Paul II helped the ninety-year-old man up and gave him his cardinal's hat. Nine thousand onlookers gave a thunderous seven-minute standing ovation to the elderly man who had devoted his life to his faith.

A seminarian once asked Cardinal Kung how he prayed during his thirty years of imprisonment. Kung replied that the communists had never taken away his rosary. Puzzled, the seminarian asked, 'How did you hide the rosary when you were thoroughly searched in jail?' Cardinal Kung just wriggled his ten fingers—his replacement for the ten beads in each segment of the rosary. '*Ave Maria*,' he said. 'You will always have your rosary and you will never be without Holy Mother's help.'

Our Lady is indeed the mother of our salvation.
—A MEDITATION ON THE CRUCIFIXION OF JESUS BY
CARDINAL IGNATIUS KUNG WRITTEN IN PRISON IN CHINA
(1955–1988)

The Lady with the Golden Heart
— Belgium —

In the late autumn of 1932, in the small town of Beauraing near Brussels, fifteen-year-old Fernande Voisin and her eleven-year-old brother Albert were walking to the local convent school to pick up their sister Gilberte, aged thirteen. On the way they stopped to pick up their friends and neighbours, Andrée Degeimbre, aged fourteen, and her nine-year-old sister, Gilberte. To avoid confusion between Gilberte Voisin and Gilberte Degeimbre, the Voisin girl was called Big Gilberte, while the younger Degeimbre girl was called Little Gilberte.

The four friends set out on 29 November 1932 on a misty autumn evening. A gravel pathway led to the convent's iron gate. A railway line ran nearby, crossing over a bridge. In the gardens around the convent school was a simple grotto to Our Lady of Lourdes, nestled beside a hawthorn tree. As he rang the convent bell, Albert glanced towards the familiar grotto. An unfamiliar sight met his eyes.

'Look! The Virgin, dressed in white, is walking above the bridge!' he cried, pointing in excitement. His older sister did not even bother to turn around. She herself had played a similar prank herself before. 'Be quiet, silly,' she said. 'It's the headlights of a car.' But Albert insisted, so the three girls turned their heads and saw the image that would change their lives forever.

Above the bridge, a shining female figure in white glided through the air, her feet hidden by a small cloud. When Sister Valeria answered the door, the children cried: 'Sister, the Virgin is walking above the grotto! She's all in white. We're frightened!'

'It's a branch waving in the wind,' she reassured them. Even when she turned on the garden lights, she could see nothing. 'You've made a mistake; a statue can't move.'

Gilberte Voisin peered out from behind the nun; she too, could see the glowing lady. But Sister Valerie seemed oblivious. Terrified, all five children ran away. Albert and Fernande ran ahead, with Andrée and Gilberte Voisin holding the hands of little Gilberte. But it was too much for her, and she tripped over, crying. As they paused, the other four looked back. The glowing figure still hovered in the air.

When the children reached the Degeimbre home their story was met with great scepticism. At the Voisin household they had much the same response. But despite their terror, the young visionaries slept soundly that night. There had been something deeply mesmerising about what they'd seen. They had half-wanted to stay a little longer with the lady, for she was very beautiful.

By morning, excitement had overcome their fear, and soon the children were telling their tale to anyone who would listen. No one believed them. As evening approached, the children once again took their familiar daily walk to Gilberte's school. As they walked up the gravel path, they covered their eyes, half afraid of what they might see. Big Gilberte came out to meet them this time, and as they all approached the convent gate they saw the glowing lady again.

The figure floated in the air, backwards and forwards above the bridge. This time the children did not stop to look. They took to their heels and ran away. Suspecting the children were the victims of a prankster, Madame Degeimbre decided that next time they went to the convent she would go too.

A small crowd had gathered, and the four children led it through the cobbled streets. Madame Degeimbre, armed with a big stick, walked a little way behind, figuring that if the children appeared to be walking alone the prankster might strike again and she could catch him in the act.

As they approached the gates, she told them to go on ahead while the adults had a thorough look around the grounds. The children went through the gates, Big Gilberte came out to meet them and suddenly, there above the grotto of Our Lady of Lourdes, was the shining woman, crowned by golden rays encircling her face. The children's cries soon brought the adults running. Closer than before, Mary turned to smile at the children, then vanished.

Next evening, Madame Degeimbre made sure she was with the children, along with Madame Voisin and a neighbour. It was around 8 p.m., and the darkness was penetrated only by Madame Degeimbre's electric torch. They were only a few metres from the convent gates when the children dropped to their knees on the cobblestone path. It was as though their legs gave way beneath them. From that time on they would always greet Mary this way, and though they often hit the ground with great speed and force, sometimes tearing their stockings, they were never hurt or bruised. They would later describe the feeling as like 'kneeling on cushions'.

On this night, the children seemed to gaze intently at the crooked branch of a hawthorn tree within the convent gates. 'She is there on that branch,' insisted Andrée. Overcome by tears, she could only add, 'How beautiful she is.'

Madame Degeimbre began to walk towards the tree. 'Stop!' cried Andrée, 'You are going to tread on her!' Madame Degeimbre later said, 'It was then that I began to believe the children.'

It wasn't only the children's parents who were sceptical. Several nuns accused them of being mischievous 'Bernadettes', impersonators of the saintly visionary of Lourdes. Others were certain that the children had only seen car headlights or the lamps of trains crossing the bridge. The older children received the harshest criticism. They were scolded for not controlling the wild imaginations of the younger children, or for leading them astray with fantasies. The mother superior of the convent, Mother Théophile, forbade the schoolchildren to discuss the matter. Some nuns were a little more light-hearted. One jokingly claimed that *she* was the apparition, caught wandering about the convent gardens.

A couple of nights later, as the visits continued, Albert spoke to the vision. 'Are you the Immaculate Virgin?' he asked.

The lady responded with only a slight inclination of the head as she spread open her arms.

'What do you want us to do?' he said.

Her answer was simple, almost childlike. In French she replied, 'Always be good.'

With one voice, they sang out, 'Yes, we'll always be good!' The children were excited. 'You must believe us now,' they said to the adults, 'for even if you couldn't see her you must have heard her.'

But they hadn't heard her. The other witnesses were blind to Mary's presence. They could only see and hear the responses of the children, who sounded as if they were talking to an imaginary friend.

The adults concluded that Mary was appearing only to children. To test the theory a local man, Monsieur Marischal, used his son Leopold as a guinea pig, rousing the poor child from his sleep to take him into the cold streets with the visionaries. When they arrived at the gate and saw the Blessed Virgin, the five friends dropped to their knees. The sleepy Leopold also knelt, a few moments after the others.

'Do you see anything?' asked his father.

'Nothing at all,' was the bewildered child's reply.

But the other children were lost in a different world. Gilberte Voisin described the apparition. She was wearing 'a white dress shot with blue, as if it were reflecting something blue. The hem of her dress hides her feet and mingles with the white cloud on which she stands. Her hands are clasped together and she either looks to the sky or gazes at us. She smiles and she has a white veil on her head which falls over her shoulders and comes nearly to her knees. There are rays of light all around her head, very straight and narrow. They are all the same size and look as if they are coming from her head.'

Madame Voisin, by now convinced of the apparition's authenticity, visited Mother Superior Théophile and recounted a serious conversation between her husband and their elder daughter. 'Yesterday we took Fernande aside and her father talked to her. He said: "You must tell me the truth and nothing but the truth. You are putting us all into a very serious position. If it is ever proved that you have been lying and that there's not a word of truth in your stories, you'll be finished and without any possibility of a decent future. We shall be despised and ridiculed. Everyone will laugh at us. You must think seriously about this. Now tell me what really happened."

'Unwavering, Fernande replied, "I can't say anything different from what I've already said. We have seen the Blessed Virgin, and that is all there is to it. You can hit me if you wish. You could even kill me, but I should still say that I had seen the Blessed Virgin."'

For the fourth night of apparitions, a great crowd gathered, including many sick people eager for a miracle. The children asked Mary to heal some of them, but she did not respond, by word or gesture. When they questioned her, she said that they would see her again on the feast of the Immaculate Conception, 8 December. She also said she wanted a chapel built.

Later that night, Monsieur Voisin met the parents of twelve-year-old Paulette Dereppe. For three years she had suffered from a crippling bone infection, which left her with fragile bones and open sores. When he heard of her suffering, he immediately suggested she come to the convent gates. When Monsieur Voisin, young Albert and the Dereppes returned to the apparition site that same night, a crowd of about thirty people were still there. Joining them, Albert began to pray, reciting the Hail Mary over and over again. Then he dropped to his knees—Mary had appeared. He asked Mary to heal Paulette. A moment later, Albert smiled. Although Mary had said nothing, he was confident that all would be well. 'Paulette will be cured,' he said confidently. 'The Virgin smiled so sweetly when I asked her.'

After that night Paulette received no more medical treatment. She visited the apparition site every evening, taking sips of water stirred with a piece of the hawthorn tree. But the miraculous cure still eluded her. There was no change in her condition.

Then, about two months later, on 15 February, a dramatic change occurred that seemed to make things worse. While praying the rosary at the hawthorn tree, Paulette's decaying leg was filled with such intense pain that she had to be carried home. The awful pain kept her awake until almost 3 a.m. That morning, when her father checked her bandaged leg, a large open sore had been replaced by a scar. On further examination they discovered that *all* her open wounds had been replaced by scar tissue. Miraculously, years of pain and horror had begun to heal in just a few hours.

The rapid healing continued. Soon the girl who had spent so much of her life bedridden was up and as active as any other girl her age. By May she managed to cycle nearly twenty miles in one day. Her illness had left her, and it never returned.

Mary's appearances continued, and the crowds grew. The children would drop to their knees and recite the Hail Mary in ethereal, united voices. Onlookers said that the children spoke swiftly, with loud, piercing voices. One witness called it 'unforgettable', and said, 'I'd never heard anything like it before. It seemed to penetrate to the very depths of one's soul.' The strange, deep prayers became part of every apparition, as did the sudden, violent kneeling. The children were not always united in what they saw or heard. There were times when some heard her speak, but others didn't. Sometimes some of the children didn't see her at all.

During one December apparition a priest, Father Maes, kept close to the children to observe their faces. At the moment of Mary's appearance, four of the children dropped to their knees immediately, and their voices changed as they prayed. Albert knelt a little more slowly, and with more caution, to avoid grazing his knees. He seemed to look in the same direction as the others, but his voice remained unchanged, not taking the same loud, piercing tone that it often did during apparitions. Father Maes' suspicions were raised immediately. When questioned later, the poor boy collapsed in tears. 'I did not see her,' he admitted. And it was terrible, he said, to feel apart from her.

The others all gave the same simple description. 'Our Lady was small. She seemed not more than four feet tall. She looked very young and extremely beautiful and spoke with a very soft and gentle voice. She stood outlined as sharply as an ordinary person or a statue. She shone with a light that was brilliant, yet it was a light that never dazzled.'

The children were the subjects of a thorough investigation. During the apparitions, they were burned by matches, pinched, and pricked with the blade of a penknife. Doctors would take their pulse and shine torches in their eyes. When the children were under Mary's influence, these tests seemed to have no ill effects on them. They seemed oblivious to all around them, except their Virgin. They were in a state of heightened ecstasy.

The Virgin Mary visited the children thirty-three times between November 1932 and January 1933. Each time the crowds grew, as did the reports of miracles. Mary would speak simply, and in few words, often responding to questions asked by the children under prompting from adults. She sometimes gave simple instructions, such as their next meeting time. When asked what she wanted, she replied simply, 'A chapel.' On 23 December, when Fernande asked why she had come, Mary replied, 'So that people will come here on pilgrimages.'

Mother Théophile, who had always been suspicious, wanted to be sure that the apparitions were truly of Mary, not a more sinister supernatural force in disguise. As Saint Benedict's medal is known to ward off evil forces, she attached one to the branch of the hawthorn tree where Mary was most often seen.

For a few days she did not appear, and Mother Théophile's doubts seemed confirmed. Then, on 27 December, Mary returned at the unusual time of 10 p.m. The children had come to the convent gardens earlier that night, but after praying, they went home, resigned to not seeing Mary for yet another night. Little Gilberte Degeimbre couldn't sleep and had a headache. At 9.30 p.m., she pleaded to return to the apparition site. The parents consented, the other children went with her, and soon all five were reunited with Mary.

The next night, the accounts of the visionaries differed more than usual. While Fernande heard nothing, Gilberte Voisin heard only the words 'last appearance', Gilberte Degeimbre heard, 'It will soon be the last time I come,' and Andrée and Albert heard, 'It will soon be my last appearance.' However, although the words varied, the message was clear.

The following night, 29 December, a crowd of 8000 gathered at the convent. Mary appeared at the usual time but, after about two dozen Hail Marys, she vanished. Seeing that the children didn't speak, the doctors present assumed that they hadn't communicated with Mary, so they decided not to hold the usual interview with the children afterwards.

But Fernande insisted. 'You must question us,' she cried. 'Something new happened. I saw something new. When the Virgin opened her arms before disappearing, she had a heart.' A shining, golden heart, surrounded by rays of brilliant light. But only Fernande saw it.

The next night, Andrée and Gilberte Voisin also saw the golden heart. But only Fernande heard Mary's words: 'Pray, pray a great deal.' The night after that, all five children saw the heart. 'Pray without ceasing,' Mary said to Gilberte Voisin.

The final apparition came on 3 January. About 30,000 people had gathered. It was a cold, grey night, and a light rain fell steadily. It seemed a suitably sombre atmosphere for the farewell, which the children had been dreading since Mary had warned them of it the night before.

When she appeared, they fell to their knees—except for Fernande, who saw nothing. The vision faded, and the children got up to leave. Fernande could not bring herself to go. 'I want to see her,' she pleaded. So she was allowed to remain in the gardens.

Ninety doctors and thirty other witnesses interrogated the children. Mary had told some of them private secrets; these the children would not divulge. Little Gilberte Degeimbre would say only that Mary had said 'farewell', and the words, 'This is between you and me and I ask of you to speak of it to no one.' To Andrée, Mary had simply said, 'I am the Mother of God, the Queen of Heaven. Pray always,' and 'Farewell'. To Gilberte Voisin, she also bade farewell, said, 'I shall convert sinners', and confided a secret that Gilberte would not reveal. Gilberte had noticed that Mary seemed brighter than usual and smiled more.

Albert was similarly tight lipped. 'She spoke, but forbade me to tell you what she said and I won't tell you,' he said. When asked if this message was sad or cheerful, he said 'Sad.' 'For whom?' asked his interrogators. 'For me,' the boy replied.

Outside, poor Fernande waited and waited. Many of the adults stayed with her. They heard a thunderous, explosive sound and saw a dramatic flash of light. At that moment, Fernande finally saw Mary. She dropped to her knees, praying and sobbing.

'Do you love my son?' Mary asked. Fernande replied, 'Yes.'

'Do you love me?' she went on. 'Yes,' said Fernande. 'Then sacrifice yourself for me.' And with those cryptic words, she spread her arms. 'Farewell.'

How should I sacrifice myself? Fernande wondered. By devoting my life to prayer as a nun? By becoming a missionary? But Mary had disappeared. 'When I realised that I should never see her again in this world I began to cry.'

After the apparitions ended, the two families struggled to stay 'ordinary' despite the intrusions of curious interrogators and pleading pilgrims. The children remained devoted to Mary for the rest of their lives. All of them married and had families of their own. Some travelled, some stayed in Beauraing. Gilberte Degeimbre, the youngest, is the only surviving visionary. She married, had two children and moved to Italy. She still visits Beauraing occasionally.

And Fernande Voisin's 'sacrifice'? She married, had five children and, after a quiet life, died in 1979.

The investigations at Beauraing continued, and so did the miracles. The Voisin parents, both lapsed Catholics, returned to the faith. For Gilberte Voisin, one of the more pious of the children, this was a particularly meaningful answer to her prayers.

One of the most dramatic cures happened to Marie Van Laer. Afflicted with a degenerative disease, she was covered with tumours, virtually paralysed, and often bedridden. Five pilgrimages to Lourdes had yielded no improvement. A few months after the apparitions ended, she persuaded her family to take her to Beauraing. She was just thirty-three, and close to death. She visited Gilberte Degeimbre, who urged her to stay by the hawthorn tree where Mary had appeared so many times before.

Lying on her stretcher before the tree, Marie felt a tremendous and sudden happiness. Her pain was leaving her. She sat up, as she hadn't for years, to write a postcard to her family. The five children arrived and together they prayed the rosary. As Marie was driven away, Gilberte encouraged her. 'Have confidence. If you are not cured here, you still may be when you are back at home.'

The day after she got home, Marie began to walk. The tumours were gone, and her swollen leg had come down to a normal size. 'There's nothing more to be done,' said her doctor after examining her. 'She's cured.'

Marie's next trip to Beauraing was in thanksgiving. She joined the Franciscan Sisters of the Holy Family, and led a healthy, active life, caring for others as she had once been cared for.

Today pilgrims continue to flock to the shrine at Beauraing, eager to pray to the golden-hearted lady who calls all people to love and healing.

Our Lady of Beauraing, Immaculate Virgin,
Carry to Jesus, your son, all the intentions which we confide
to you this day. Mother with the golden heart, mirror of the
tenderness of the Father,
Look with love upon the men and women of our time
And fill them with the joy of your presence . . .
  —Prayer to Our Lady of Beauraing

My Devotion

Our Lady has a very special place on the island of Mauritius. Her shrine is situated at the foot of Signal Mountain, in the capital. Here she overlooks the port and the city of Port-Louis, protecting the nation. Her statue as Queen of Peace stands majestically above an outdoor altar, surrounded by terraced rose gardens.

I was born in Mother Bartelmy Street, across the road from the church. Our front gate faced the side entrance of the church. My parents called me Marie because I was born on the 25th of March, the feast of Our Lady's Annunciation.

On special days, like my first holy communion, we'd dress up. I was seven, and it was a bright Saturday afternoon. We'd visit friends and family, and hand out brioches (a sweet bun with a cross on it). The families brought them to the church in baskets the day before to be blessed.

On the Sunday afternoon of my confirmation, there was a procession of all the children together with parents, friends and the rest of the congregation. The girls all wore a garland of fresh white flowers on their heads, the boys carried theirs, and all the way we said the rosary and sang songs of praise to Our Lady. After a brief ceremony, each child would offer their garland to Our Lady. I can still remember a few lines of the song we sang while offering the flowers: 'Please take these flowers that I am offering to you. One day you will give them back to me in heaven.'

As a child, I always remember going there for novenas with my mam, and midnight Mass at the shrine was out of this world.

But though a lot has changed now, I still make it a point to stop there every time I go home for a holiday.

Our Lady has had and still has a deep impact in my life. Whenever I feel lost, blue or fed up, I always ask her to wrap me up in her mantle of peace so that I may find comfort and strength to go on.

—Marie, *Western Australia*

The Virgin of the Poor
— Belgium —

For eleven-year-old Mariette Beco, a glance outside her kitchen window changed her life forever. Mariette's home was a humble little house on the outskirts of Banneux-Notre-Dame, 15 kilometres southeast of Liège, near the Dutch and German borders. The small village was in one of the poorest areas of Belgium and the Beco home lay on its outskirts, at the edge of a towering pine forest.

It was a windy, snowy Sunday evening in early 1933, and Mariette, the eldest child, was sitting with her mother and the baby, waiting for her ten-year-old brother to come home. Peering through the window for some sign of him, Mariette caught sight of a strange figure. It was a young woman, with a gentle smile. Ringed by a soft oval of light, she wore a dazzling white dress with a high collar, and a sweeping gown falling elegantly in long, broad pleats. A sky-blue sash was tied about her waist, and on her head there was a transparent white veil. Mariette turned away to rub her eyes and adjust her lamp, assuming it was a trick of the light. But when she turned back, the woman was still there. Her hands were clasped and pointing downwards in a personal, familiar way. Mariette's mother laughed it off. 'Perhaps it's the Blessed Virgin,' she quipped.

Mariette did not laugh, and insisted instead that her mother come and look. When Madame Beco peered through the window, she caught a glimpse of an indistinct, glowing figure dressed in white. Thinking it was a ghost or witch, she was terrified. Mariette grabbed her rosary beads and began to pray. Then she saw the young woman's lips move, gesturing to Mariette to come to her. When Mariette asked her mother for permission to follow the lady, Madame Beco flatly refused and securely fastened the door. When Mariette next peered out the window, the figure was gone. Her brother returned home a short time later, and no word about the incident was spoken. The family went to sleep.

At school the next day, Mariette related the story to her friend Josephine during morning recess. Josephine thought she was joking and laughed, teasing Mariette until she broke down in tears. Seeing Mariette cry certainly grabbed Josephine's attention. Mariette was a practical, sturdy, tomboyish sort of girl, not one to get upset so easily. Josephine advised Mariette to see the local priest. So after school the two girls found themselves at the presbytery of Father Louis Jamin.

The conservative young priest heard the story with some scepticism. The last of the apparitions at Beauraing, only 80 kilometres away, had been reported only twelve days before Mariette's encounter. Mariette's family rarely went to church, and Mariette had been told off for missing catechism classes so often that she'd stopped attending them. Like many Belgian families, they had become disillusioned with the Church, associating the institution with the bourgeoisie, whom they saw as out of touch with the needs of the poor during the Great Depression.

Father Jamin suspected that the girl had seen the statue of Our Lady of Lourdes in their church, and based her 'vision' on that image. He tried subtly to get her to admit it. Mariette stomped her foot on the floor at the priest's scepticism. 'I know well what I've seen,' she insisted. 'I am sure of it!' It seemed likely that she had heard romantic stories of Mary and imagined one of her own. So the priest advised her to keep quiet about the matter and sent her away.

He watched Mariette carefully over the next few days. To

his surprise, she started coming much more frequently to Mass and catechism class, participating as best she could. She seemed sincere. But while he was impressed by her efforts, he remained unconvinced that any extraordinary event had occurred.

On 18 January, at around 7 p.m., Mariette slipped quietly out of her house and into the darkness. It was another cold and frosty evening. This was particularly odd behaviour for Mariette, as she was frightened of the dark. But she didn't disappear unnoticed, for the priest wasn't the only one watching Mariette closely. Her father Julien had grown curious about Mariette's story after his experiments with an oil lamp failed to reproduce her apparition. Julien followed Mariette and watched her as she knelt by the edge of the path leading to their home. She began to pray the rosary, stretching out her arms to apparent nothingness.

As Mariette knelt in the bitter cold she saw a spectacular sight. There in the sky, above the dark forest, was a woman. This lovely stranger was tiny at first, but as Mariette watched she grew in size, as if approaching at a rapid rate, until she stopped just above the ground near Mariette. She was dressed in a white robe and veil with a blue sash around her waist, and her feet rested in a small, grey cloud. Short rays of light encircled her head, and a white beaded rosary hung from her right hand. Her right foot was exposed, revealing a single golden rose.

Mariette's father watched his eldest daughter kneeling in the cold and dark. 'You're going crazy!' he told her crossly, but she showed no signs of hearing him. Disquieted, he didn't want to touch her, so he raced off on his bicycle to fetch the priest. Father was out, so he went to fetch a neighbour and his young son. They came with him immediately. By then Mariette had moved, following the figure as it moved backwards, gesturing to her to follow.

Oblivious to her audience, Mariette followed the figure

right onto the road. The others called to her, 'Where are you going? Come back!' but Mariette was deeply distracted. 'She is calling me,' she said, and continued to follow the figure that only she could see.

The lady stopped twice, and Mariette responded immediately, falling to her knees with a thump on the hard, icy ground. The lady came to a final halt over the bank of a ditch, in front of a little brook. 'Put your hands in the water,' she told Mariette. 'This spring is reserved for me.'

With these words she retreated the same way she came, rising backwards into the air until she vanished. Mariette rose slowly, as if awakening from a dream. Her father took her hand and brought her home, listening as his daughter described her incredible experience. She went to bed, and her father, still troubled, went straight to Father Jamin. Accompanied by another priest, they came to the house to find Mariette fast asleep.

The next day the priest relayed the whole story to his bishop, and that evening Mariette again took to the cold night air. Her father followed, and the figure appeared as before. It was again 7 p.m. This time Mariette spoke to her lady and asked who she was.

'I am the Virgin of the poor,' she replied, taking Mariette again to the same cold brook as the night before. Mariette continued to question her. 'You said yesterday that "this spring is reserved for me". Why for me?'

The lady smiled and laughed at Mariette's confusion. 'This stream is reserved for all nations,' she explained. 'It is to ease the sick. I will pray for you.'

That night, Mariette was heavily interrogated. But she had many questions of her own. She was grateful to see Our Lady, but she had trouble understanding her. She only grasped the meaning of the word 'nations' after she was shown a map of the world.

Mariette didn't get much sleep, so she stayed in bed the next day. Her parents didn't want her to pray in the garden that evening. Mariette threatened to jump out the window if she wasn't allowed out. At a quarter to seven she rose, dressed and went into the garden.

'Ah, there she is!' cried Mariette excitedly. 'What do you want, my beautiful lady?'

Mary smiled and replied, 'I should like a small chapel.' Mariette watched as the lady made the sign of the cross in the air. Then the little girl collapsed, unconscious. She was carried indoors and put to bed, where she recovered almost immediately.

It would be three weeks before Mariette saw Mary again. The girl knelt faithfully in her garden every night, praying the rosary. Sometimes she was alone, sometimes neighbours came. On one occasion a group of youths taunted her. She endured constant teasing from friends, neighbours and family members, particularly her grandmother and her aunts. Children would mockingly genuflect before her, call her Bernadette, after the visionary of Lourdes, and do crude impressions of the Virgin Mary. On one occasion she was badly beaten. Few visionaries had suffered so much.

Then, on 11 February, the feast of Our Lady of Lourdes, Mariette's prayers were answered. Mary reappeared and led her to the brook. Mariette fell to her knees and dipped her hand into the spring, blessing herself. '*Je viens soulager la souffrance*,' the lady said in French. 'I come to relieve suffering.' And she left again, leaving Mariette overwhelmed and in tears. She asked her father to translate the French words into their Belgian dialect, Walloon. Even then she did not quite know what 'relieve' meant. Mariette suspected that it was a good thing, for the lady had smiled. She only knew her beloved lady had left, and she missed her. History would give additional meaning to Mary's words; she had appeared only twelve days after Adolf Hitler came to power in Germany.

When Our Lady next appeared, four days later, Mariette was feeling the pressure of the sceptics all around her. Father Jamin demanded proof of the apparitions. 'Blessed Virgin, the priest has told me to ask you to give us a sign,' she told her.

'Believe in me,' Mary replied simply, 'I shall believe in you. Pray a great deal.' Mary repeated this advice three times. She then told Mariette a secret, leaving her in tears once again. The girl kept the secret faithfully, though many people interrogated her afterwards. 'You can kill me just like you do the rabbits,' she cried. 'Even then I would not tell it!'

The next evening Mariette knelt in the snow, praying the rosary as she waited for Mary. Suddenly the speed and loudness of her prayers increased dramatically. Mary had appeared, and once again she led Mariette to the brook. 'My dear child, pray a great deal,' she insisted. Mariette wept, 'because she left too quickly'.

The final apparition came ten days later. Heavy rain had been falling all afternoon, but Mariette knelt in the garden, praying the rosary in the rain as a woman held an umbrella over her. The group of witnesses said two whole rosaries before the showers cleared and bright stars emerged in the deep-blue sky.

This time Mary seemed sorrowful. 'I am the Mother of the Saviour, Mother of God,' she said. 'Pray a great deal. Adieu.' She placed her hands on Mariette, blessing her and making the sign of the cross. And as she departed over the pine trees for the final time, Mariette threw herself to the ground, weeping and praying Hail Marys in between bursts of sobbing.

'The Blessed Virgin will not come again,' she mourned. 'She said farewell.'

Mary's request was fulfilled, and a small chapel was built in her honour. It soon became a centre of pilgrimage, faith and healing for all nations, just as Mary had promised. Similar shrines have since been built all over the world, in Brazil, France, Romania, Holland, the Belgian Congo, Germany, Austria, India and Italy. A larger church, several religious orders, retreat houses and facilities for the poor and needy have also been established at Banneux. The flags of all nations adorn the shrine, as a reminder of Our Lady's gift to all peoples. And little plaques in the street mark each point where Mariette stopped and knelt before Mary, as she led the girl to the spring.

Not many people were present at Mariette's apparitions, perhaps no more than forty during the whole period of the appearances. Nevertheless, news of them spread. In 2006, about half a million pilgrims visited Banneux. Its facilities have been adapted to welcome the sick and the disabled, allowing Mary's blessings to be accessible to all, as she had asked. In 2008, the shrine celebrated the seventy-fifth anniversary of the apparitions.

As for Mariette, she dedicated herself to the care of the sick and needy pilgrims who visited the shrine. She eventually married and had a family of her own. She is now eighty-seven years old and has withdrawn from the world, living quietly near Banneux. She encountered Mary eight times, but always saw herself as a mere instrument of grace.

'My mission was like that of a postman who delivers mail,' she said. 'Now I have delivered the message given to me by the Virgin. And like a postman I want to slip away after delivering the mail, I want to withdraw in peace and prayer without anyone disturbing me.'

Mariette's last public appearance was in May 1985, when Pope John Paul II visited the apparition site and met with her. She rarely returns to the place now. Her work there is finished. For many others, Banneux is a centre for healing and grace, a place where the Virgin of the Poor grants all nations the gift of new life.

Virgin of the Poor, save all nations
Virgin of the Poor, relieve the suffering
Virgin of the Poor, we believe in you.
—Prayer to the Virgin of the Poor, Banneux

A Short Story of Healing and Peace

I went to Banneux on pilgrimage in May 2002, then visited my mother, who had been suffering through a long illness. I sprinkled her with the water of Banneux, even putting some water on her tongue, which was very dry. My mother passed away the next night. I am convinced that the Blessed Virgin Mary took her, putting an end to her suffering. It was a beautiful way for her to leave this world.

—Martina, *Western Australia*

An Artist's Miracle

I am an artist and I worked on a mural painting of Mother Mary for a shrine in Yankalilla, a small town just south of Adelaide. I had a couple of amazing experiences while painting it.

I had undertaken the work without pay. One afternoon, while paying some bills, I was fretting about my finances, but something told me to just let go! When I arrived home there was an envelope sticking out from under the welcome mat, with my name written on it. When

I opened it, I found no explanation or name, just five new $100 bills! I phoned around, including to the church, but nobody I called knew anything about it. I just thought, Wow! Miracles do happen!

The next experience happened when I started painting Mary's face. I had meditated and prayed for guidance and as I started on her eyes, it felt as if a piece of the sun had entered my heart, illuminating it and quickening its beat till my whole body started shaking. I felt as if I had been given a tiny piece of the world's sorrows and joys to experience simultaneously, and I burst into tears. I had to stop what I was doing to 'mop up' and start again. But the same thing happened again. The priest and another lady entered the room and said I was having a spiritual experience. I turned to them, sobbing, and said, 'I know!' They took me to their place, where the whole thing started again; the feelings came in intermittent waves for the rest of the day. The lady took my pulse and noticed a change in my heart rate. It was the most awesome, incredibly beautiful experience I have ever had!

—Marie, *South Australia*

Mary of the Snows
— Italy —

The miracle of Our Lady of the Snows dates back to the year 352. An elderly Roman couple prayed to Mary for guidance on how to spend their fortune, as they had no heir.

One night she appeared, telling them to build a church in her honour on Esquiline Hill. She said she would indicate the exact location using snow. The couple were amazed, as it was August, one of the hottest months of the year. Snow is rare in Rome, even in winter, and many seasons pass without so much as a flake. That night Pope Liberius received the same message from Mary in a vivid dream.

On the morning of 5 August, an astonished crowd gathered at Esquiline Hill. In the middle of summer, it gleamed white. When the couple and the Pope arrived at the site, they discovered a vast expanse covered in snow that formed the outline of a great church. As soon as the measurements were recorded, the snow disappeared. Now the couple knew what they were called to do, and they donated the funds for the church that would become known as the Basilica of St Mary Major. This answer to a childless couple's prayer is said to be the oldest church dedicated to Mary in the west, the mother of all churches dedicated to Mary around the world.

Each year the 5 August anniversary is still commemorated with a shower of white flower petals from the dome of the chapel, sprinkled during Mass and Vespers. They fall at the words: 'He sendeth his snow like wool . . .' White jasmine symbolises the purity and innocence of Mary, and rose petals represent the mystical rose herself.

Within the basilica, an ancient Byzantine icon is venerated in the Borghese Chapel. It was supposedly brought to Rome by Saint Helena, the mother of Constantine, the first Christian emperor. The painting, said to be the work of Saint Luke the Evangelist, saved Rome twice, once from plague in the year 604, and again during a cholera epidemic just over 1200 years later. It soon became known as *Salus Populi Romani*, Health of the Roman People and protectoress of the city.

One miraculous story, dating back to the year 597, tells of a terrible plague. Entire families were wiped out. Pope Gregory the Great led the icon in prayerful procession to Hadrian's tomb. As the crowd came to the ancient site, a heavenly choir was heard singing in Latin: 'Queen of Heaven, rejoice, alleluia; for he whom you did merit to bear, alleluia; has risen as he said, alleluia.'

The pilgrims were astonished. The Pope, greatly moved, cried to Mary: 'Pray for us to God, alleluia.'

At that moment the Archangel Michael, traditional defeater of evil, appeared over Hadrian's tomb with sword drawn. He returned his sword to its sheath in a powerful symbolic gesture. The plague had been defeated. The people left, rejoicing in the certainty that their prayers had been answered. From that moment on, Hadrian's tomb became known as Castel Sant'Angelo. The prayer taught by the angels, *Regina Coeli*, Queen of Heaven, is still sung today.

Copies of this miraculous icon spread far and wide. In each country, the image changed slightly to reflect new cultures. The original image came to be known as Our Lady of the Snow, or Lady of the Snows, for its association with the miraculous church in Italy. In the Bavarian seminary of Ingolstadt, Germany, the image became known as the Mater Admirabilis, later, the Mater ter Admirabilis, Mother Thrice Admirable. In

China, it became known as the Madonna of Singanfu. A 16th-century Chinese copy is now kept in the Chicago Field Museum of National History.

Devotion to Mary as Our Lady of the Snows was taken to the American midwest in 1941 by Father Paul Schulte, known as 'the flying priest of the Arctic'. A priest of the Missionary Oblates of Mary Immaculate, he would fly his plane to remote missions deep into the Arctic, bringing medical aid and supplies. Through his work he developed a strong personal devotion to Our Lady of the Snows.

Father Paul commissioned an artist, J. Watson Davis, to create a painting of Our Lady of the Snows that also showed a missionary priest flying his plane to the aid of an Inuit mission. In it, Our Lady of the Snows is surrounded by the glowing rays of the Aurora Borealis, the Northern Lights.

After his work in the Arctic, Father Paul settled at St Henry's Seminary in Belleville, Illinois, and the painting was hung in the seminary chapel. Its influence continued to grow, and local devotion to Mary eventually blossomed into a perpetual novena to Our Lady of the Snows.

When a new chapel was built at the seminary, it included a special side chapel for the painting. The first solemn outdoor novena was held in 1951, concluding on 5 August, the feast of Our Lady of the Snows. The novena became an annual event and soon pilgrims were coming in the thousands.

Eventually the modest chapel became too small for the many pilgrims. The Missionary Oblates of Mary Immaculate looked for a more suitable location. Several years later, they found it: eighty acres of farmland on the bluffs overlooking the Mississippi River.

An association of ordinary people with a devotion to Mary, was formed. They bought twenty more acres, and the construction of a great shrine began in earnest. Today the National Shrine of Our Lady of the Snows sits on over 200 acres, and more than a million people visit it each year. The painting of the flying priest and the Lady of the Snows hangs in the visitor's centre lobby. In the church, a new icon of Our Lady of the Snows was placed.

Today Our Lady of the Snows has become a pilgrim icon in one of the world's largest pilgrimages, World Youth Day. Young pilgrims gather in a chosen nation for a week of prayer and devotion culminating in Mass with the Pope. Millions gather at every event, and the atmosphere is electric. As Our

Lady of the Snows was painted as a Hodigitria, or guiding icon, she is a most suitable leader to gather the youth of the world in prayer.

Pope John Paul II first gave a contemporary copy of the icon to a group of young people from Cologne in 2003, in anticipation of the great World Youth Day event to be held there in 2005. 'Today I also entrust to you . . . the icon of Mary,' he told them. 'From now on it will accompany the World Youth Days, together with the Cross . . . It will be a sign of Mary's motherly presence close to young people who are called . . . to welcome her into their lives.'

Since that day, the icon copy of Our Lady of the Snows has travelled on every World Youth Day pilgrimage.

Our Lady was present in the cenacle with the Apostles as they waited for Pentecost. May she be your mother and guide. May she teach you to receive the word of God, to treasure it and to ponder on it in your heart, as she did throughout her life.

—POPE BENEDICT XVI

A Modern Pilgrim's Story

I was taught to love Mary from a young age. My mother taught me how to pray the rosary, and together we would pray in thanksgiving, or in times of difficulty, for big or small reasons or for no reason at all. Even when I was in primary school, we would pray before my school exams. And Our Lady always comforted me, even in the simplest ways.

In 2002 I had the wonderful opportunity of going to World Youth Day in Toronto, Canada. It was an incredible week, exhausting but uplifting. I was booked to return home via the US and New Zealand. I wasn't looking forward to that eleven-hour US–New Zealand flight, but at least I'd be with friends. If I ever got to the end of the long queues . . .

It was twenty minutes to boarding time when I finally made it to the front of the immigration line. Then I was stopped. I was told I couldn't get on to the plane to the US. I couldn't believe it.

During my one week in Canada, the American laws had changed. Indonesian passport holders like me needed a visa to get into the US. Even though I had Australian permanent residency, I couldn't take a single step onto US soil, even if it was just in an airport.

I protested, to no avail. I was sent to apply for a transfer-without-permit visa. Meanwhile my fellow pilgrims were boarding the plane that would take them briefly to the US, then home. There was no way I could make that flight. After the paperwork was sorted out, a security guard escorted me to the next available plane from Toronto. A bit of calculation told me that I would be arriving in Los Angeles with enough time to board the plane to New Zealand and rejoin my group. But a snowstorm delayed my plane for two hours. I couldn't believe my luck. The chances of missing that connecting flight were getting greater and greater. I didn't mind making an eleven-hour flight on my own, but it would be nice to spend it with my fellow pilgrims and friends! With nowhere left to turn, I took out my rosary beads and prayed. It was an impossible request, but I prayed for it anyway: Please, Mary, let me catch up with the others somehow. Only Mary could help me now!

When the plane stopped, I was the first to disembark. In what was possibly the quickest connection in aeronautical history, I raced from one plane to the next, which was parked beside mine. On the crowded plane I saw my first familiar face: my friend Craig. And beside him, the Archbishop of Perth, Western Australia!

My pilgrim friends had kicked up a fuss on my behalf. I had been unable to tell any of them about the visa fiasco, but they noticed immediately that I was missing. The plane was delayed in Toronto for at least half an hour as the staff checked the records for the passenger whose name had been electronically removed from the list. When they realised what had happened, they were finally able to depart, giving my stormbound plane the time I needed to catch up with them.

The pilgrims were seated at the very back. I was the last passenger to board. When they saw me walking in, the whole plane erupted with applause. It was a miracle. Mary made sure her wayward pilgrim would continue his path with his companions.

—Daryl, *Western Australia*

Mary, Queen of Arabia
— Kuwait —

Father Theophano Stella was a strong-willed and entrepreneurial man. As the first resident priest of Kuwait, he had to be. An Italian priest in a non-Christian land, he was shepherd to a small community. He needed something to focus people's love and prayer. He needed Mary.

An old power station in the port of Ahmadi was converted into a chapel in 1948, and a framed picture of Mary was brought from Mount Carmel and placed inside. Father Stella eventually decided to have a statue built for Mary under the new title of Our Lady of Arabia. It was carved from a solid block of Lebanese cedar. Devotion to Our Lady of Arabia soon spread, and many people gathered to pray before the statue.

Ahmadi was a centre of oil production, and many migrant workers settled there. Our Lady was a source of great comfort to them. Many fondly recall the festive atmosphere as the statue was taken in procession to the chapel.

Soon a new, grander church was built in Ahmadi. It was the first Catholic church built on Kuwaiti soil, and it was dedicated to Mary. The corner stone was taken from the ruins of an ancient church at Aylesford in Kent, England. It was a former Dominican monastery that Saint Simon Stock had established as a haven for Carmelites. From this church in Ahmadi, Our Lady of Arabia would be venerated as patroness and protector of the oilman.

A small replica was blessed by Pope Pius XII and given to young Kuwaiti pilgrims during their visit to Rome in 1954, a year dedicated to Mary. It was placed in the Holy Family Cathedral in

Kuwait City, where it sits to this day. Behind the statue, a fresco depicts the Queen of Arabia in all her glory.

One distinctive feature of Our Lady was her crown. In fact, there were two crowns, one for Mary and the other for Jesus. Finely chiselled and encrusted with diamonds, rubies and other precious stones, the crowns were fashioned from two pounds of pure gold and blessed in 1960 by Pope John XXIII. A large pearl of the Gulf, a gift from the bishop, also adorned Our Lady's head.

A cardinal representing the Pope arrived in Kuwait to crown the statue. It was the feast of the Assumption of Mary, and over forty children received their first holy communion that day. Each child was given a signed picture of the Last Supper as a memento. Then, in a ceremony in the large square in front of the church the statue was crowned during a spectacular sunset. More than 4000 people packed the large, open square, and as Our Lady of Arabia became Queen of Arabia, thunderous applause broke out in a moving display of solidarity, devotion and love.

In the following decades the Queen guided her people through all kinds of trials. In 1990, the Iraqi invasion of Kuwait devastated the entire country, including Ahmadi. The priests struggled to continue services as usual, and everyone prayed fervently for peace. The statue of Our Lady of Arabia was crushed and greatly abused. Bombs dropped on nearby houses also damaged the church. Parishioners did their best to lovingly restore the statue.

When Kuwait was liberated in 1991, the church bells rang continuously, while prayer services of thanksgiving were held in five languages. Saturday evenings continue to have a special place in Ahmadi residents' hearts. People gather together to pray the perpetual novena to Our Lady of Arabia, and the church is crammed with devotees of Mary. Twelve nationalities come to Mary in prayer—English, Australian, American, Irish, French, Indian, Pakistani, Palestinian, Lebanese, Syrian, Iraqi and Iranian. A special box is kept near the statue, filled with prayer petitions and letters of thanksgiving for graces received. In her early days, Our Lady of Arabia was the patroness of the oilman. Today she is also the patroness against terrorism. Mary remains a beacon of hope in the Arabian desert.

*Dear Mother, we call thee Our Lady of Arabia to ask for thy
blessing upon this country, and for thy loving protection on us.
Keep us ever near thy child Jesus, in the happiness of sanctify-
ing grace. Amen.*

—From a novena prayer to Our Lady of Arabia

Memories of an Arabian Queen

*I was born in Kuwait and went to live permanently in the US in my late
teens. Mum was an Irish Catholic, and my Irish grandmother was very
devout. When I was born, she sent from Ireland a tiny miraculous medal,
pinned on a cardboard heart covered in old brocade. On the back, in her
handwriting, were the words, 'To Baby, whom God is pleased to send.'
I have kept it all these years. My sister, more devout than I, thought she
did not have a medal. But as we were going through my mother's old
wooden trunk after she died, I noticed something stuck in the corner. I
pulled, and there was the little miraculous medal of my sister, discovered
decades after it was sent. My sister feels that we have been under Our
Lady's protection ever since.*

*My sister and I are very much opposites. I am plodding, methodi-
cal, rather introverted; my sister is pragmatic, decisive, and sociable.
While caring for our mother during her final illness, we complemented
each other very well. Upon her death, I was named executor of the will.
My sister wanted to go through things quickly. Since I wanted to do it
very thoroughly, I ended up with several boxes of papers, books and the
like. We figured most of it was throwaway stuff.*

*The Christmas before Mum died, 2005, I received a computer as
a present. I learned how to do web research and became curious about
Kuwait. At the time I leaned heavily on Our Lady in my grief at my
mother's passing.*

*On the internet I found the Church of Our Lady of Arabia. I had
lived in Kuwait until I was twelve, and still treasured childhood*

memories from there. I remembered kneeling in front of the statue of Our Lady and being fascinated by her crown and that of the baby Jesus, and by her beautiful blue clothing. Mostly, I remember gazing up at the statue, and being amazed at how beautiful she was. She was so pretty, gazing down on me with Jesus and the two cherubs . . . not to mention the gold crown. To a little girl who was a daydreamer, the scene was a piece of heaven on earth. It was easy to see Mary as Queen of Heaven with her benevolent smile, the cherubs and the adorable child Jesus.

On the web I read about the crowning of the statue in 1960 and the children who received their first holy communion that day. A shiver went through me, because I realised I was one of those children. I still have the slightly chipped gold-framed certificate featuring the Lord's Supper that each child was presented with on the day.

My mother was a very sensible, stoic woman. After she died, we found a tiny address book in which she had written a few sentences about important moments in her life. My mother always seemed so strong, never showed sadness, but in this book she talked about her feelings. Some of her writings were dated on my holy communion day. She took my sister and me to the crowning that evening, where we mingled with around 700 people.

'March 25th. Today Belinda made her first holy communion. She looked so lovely in her white . . . . It was a wonderful day but B is so young she doesn't really understand it all. So anxious and so good, too wonderful to see.'

It is interesting that all this happened after my mother died. I do think that grief can bring a lot of blessings, if one is open and if the person has been very close to you. There is no doubt that Our Lady had been in all our lives from day one.

My memories of Kuwait are sometimes vague, but I will never forget Our Lady of Arabia: 'Our Lady of Arabia, Star of the Gulf, pray for the Bedouin, pray for me.'

—Belinda, *United States*

Conclusion

Mary's mantle has brushed every corner of the world as she pours her love and grace on all her children. As communication speeds up and the world seems to shrink, more stories of Mary emerge, and more people deepen in their devotion to this wonderful and mysterious figure. But with the spread of information comes the need for responsibility and a discerning heart. Discernment is a keenness of insight, that helps one find the truth. Here, too, Mary is our guide. When the angel appeared to her and asked her to bear the Son of God, she didn't accept immediately. She asked questions to discern the truth, before she gave her heart and her life to it.

Discernment is essential in every experience of Mary. In all these stories there is a strong element of intuition. Sometimes people just know they are in the presence of something holy when they encounter Mary, whether they identify her immediately or not. Others are less sure. Faith and intellect need to go hand in hand if we are to understand Mary fully. Spiritual experiences are about more than just feelings, and so much can be learned if we approach them with a combination of openness and discernment. Ask questions, observe, investigate. This is an important part of every encounter with Mary, ensuring that with love of her comes some of her wisdom.

Discernment has also been important in the writing of this book. I have heard stories, researched, questioned, prayed and sometimes consulted priests and other authorities on Mary. Not every story of Mary is included here, because not every story has been fully evaluated. Some stories have been hard to exclude because at face value they are very beautiful. But below the surface they lack something. True stories of Mary have a depth and wisdom that nourishes and inspires.

Writing this book has been an amazing experience, very challenging and deeply personal. Many times I have sat down to write only to find some meaning in the date, or some connection to a personal experience. The stories of Mary through time and space interweave and intersect like the fabric of her own mantle, at once intricate, soft and consoling.

In writing this book I feel I've become a small part of that great tapestry. I can't say I'm now passionately in love with Mary. But my love for her, like all great loves, has grown gradually and my appreciation of her has deepened. It is hard not to be moved when you find yourself in a great parish hall filled with World War II refugees who genuinely believe that Mary saved their lives. Or to sit in someone's living room and watch tears well in their eyes as they tell a stranger about all their Blessed Mother has given them. Or to walk into a Coptic church, or an Orthodox church, or a Catholic church and to recognise in one corner a familiar and ancient image of Mary, a reminder of the same great devotion, so beautifully and so uniquely expressed, in faiths that have evolved through different paths over many centuries. It is like coming home again.

It's difficult to grasp the full mystery and meaning of Mary in so many lives. But I hope these pages express some sense of people's different journeys, and afford a small glimpse into Mary's remarkable, profound love.

Acknowledgements

T his book could never have been written without the support and prayers of many people.

Maggie Hamilton's vision first led me to this book, and Carmelo Musca's encouragement helped me to accept the challenge of writing it. Their continued support has been invaluable.

One of the great pleasures of writing this book has been meeting and drawing on the wisdom of some very lovely people of many different religions. Thank you to Father Brian O'Loughlin, Juliet Mascarenhas, the Vicariate Apostolic of Kuwait, Father Hugh Thomas, Father Anthony Van Dyke, Father Nektarios Serfes, Father Doug Harris, Bishop John Mackey, Bishop Hilton Deakin, Father Abram Abdelmalek, Father John Schroedel, Orthodox Wiki, Father Ron Gagné, MS, La Salette Communications Center, Father Henry Grodecki, Association of the Miraculous Medal, Father Alfonsas Savickis, Vicky and all at the Aboriginal Ministry WA, Archpriest Sergei Okunev, Father Tomas Bujakowski, Father Jesus Bello, Father Andre Mary Feain, Father Dominic Savio, Bishop Ross Davies, Father Neville Connell, Chris St John and everyone at the Society of Mary, Father Leszek Czelusniak, Sister Veronica Therese Willaway, Father Roman Wroblewski, SDS, the Carmelite Sisters at Gelorup, the Ursuline Sisters at Fremantle, the Schoenstatt Sisters at Armadale, Bishop Pat Dunn, Abbé Gilon, sanctuaires de Beauraing, Father Sunil De Silva, Archdiocese of Colombo, Basilian Fathers Latin

American Apostolate and Father Henry Grodecki, Association of the Miraculous Medal.

Thanks also to Elisabeth Econquer, MDN, M.N.K. Boulos, Wendy McKinley, Joan Peters, Joseph Kung, the Cardinal Kung Foundation, Abbot Placid, the Benedictine Community of New Norcia, Sister Zita, skete.com, Stan Kain, Phillip Apergis, aperges.com, Valentina Okunev, Ann Ball, Jennifer Jetton, the National Shrine of Our Lady of the Snows, Belleville, Illinois, Anne Milton, Roman Catholic National Shrine of Walsingham, The Anglican Shrine of Our Lady of Walsingham, the Franciscan Friars of the Immaculate, the communities of Montallegro and Monte Vergine, the Pauline communities in Australia (Marian Valley and Penrose Park), the Blue Army, World Apostolate of Fátima, USA, Megan R. Pritchard, Seitai Hoshikai Handmaids of the Eucharist community, Akita, Japan, Bishop Isao Yama Kikuchi, Archbishop Barry Hickey, Father Van Vinh Doug, Angelo Cacciola Donati, La Convivialitá, Montallegro, P.D. Benedetto OSB, Peter Macken, Monte Vergine Abbey, Abbé Joseph Cassart, Banneux, Anny De Deyn, Donal Foley, Dr Virginia Kimball, Paddy and Rita Mcgrane, Roma Martino, David de Armey, Keith Gardine, the Servants of Mary Help of Christians, Wanda Harasymow, Knock Shrine Publications, Andrei Zlate and Stephenie, Pat Lavelle, George and Rita Jacob, Eileen Davidson, my aunties Moira Selvage and Ellen Curran, Ted Harasti, and Michael P. Duricy.

And a very special thanks to Angela Handley, Kathy Mossop, Sarah Hickie, everyone at Allen & Unwin and everyone who contributed their time, effort, and stories from all over the world, many of whom have chosen to remain nameless. Thanks also to the many friends who offered their support through kind words of encouragement, proofreading and counselling, including Bronia Karniewicz, Ekaterina Lygoti, Paul Bui, Verity Gorddard, Natalie Thomas, Clare Pike, Beatrice Yong, Miller Lokanata, Daryl Pranata, Jen Grout, Anita Parker, Agata

Sadowska, Gray Hutchins, Grant Gorddard, Rachel Way, Lydia Fernandez, Yasmine and Ali Hussaini, Irene Wellm, Marianne Delouge, Brother Giles, Sister Juanita and all the lovely Catherine McAuley awardees and convenors of 2007. I am particularly indebted to my excellent research assistant, Martina Aliraja, always so enthusiastic and dedicated, who found so much wonderful material and helped translate many French texts.

Several very strong influences have also helped to make this book (and me) what it is, and to one of them, my dear grandmother Margaret (Marjorie) Mary Phillips, I have dedicated this book. From her I learned to love reading and prayer, to strive for an open, inquisitive mind and an affectionate heart. My principal devotion to Mary, as Our Lady of Perpetual Help, came through her. Three very strong Italian women have also been instrumental in forming me and my appreciation of my faith, and of Mary: my 'nonna' Celesta Azzolini, Madre Agostina Marchetti and Marisa Ferrarini, who have been like mothers to me from the other side of the world. I am sure Nonna and Madre are watching and laughing at me from high above. Also up there is my dear grandpa, Stanley Walter Phillips. Thanks to all my family, friends and work colleagues who put up with me, particularly my beloved parents Philomena Myra Curran and Peter Curran, and my poor old brother Sean who always looks after me so well. I could never have done this without them.

Thanks to all my family, friends and work colleagues who put up with me, particularly my beloved parents Philomena Myra Curran and Peter Curran. And my poor old brother Sean who had to do so much proofreading.

I could never have done this without all these people. I don't think I'll ever quite understand why I was called to write this book, but I'll always be grateful for it.

'The Blessed Virgin chose me only because
I was the most ignorant.'
—St Bernadette of Lourdes

Photo Acknowledgements

Further Reading

Attwater, Donald, *A Dictionary of Mary*, London: Longmans, Green and Co., 1957

Beevers, John, *The Sun Her Mantle*, Dublin: Browne & Nolan Ltd, 1954

Chiffolo, Anthony F., *100 Names of Mary*, Cincinnati, OH: St Anthony Messenger Press, 2001

W.D. Creede, *Make Her Known: A Redemptorist Tribute to God's Mother*, Perth: Redemptorist Monastery (booklet)

Cruz, Joan Carroll, *Miraculous Images of Our Lady*, Rockford, IL: Tan Books and Publishers, Inc., 1993

Delaney, John J. (ed.), *A Woman Clothed With the Sun*, New York: Doubleday & Company, Inc., 1961

Newton, Father Paul A., *Making Sense of Private Revelations*, Victoria, Australia: Divine Mercy Publications, 2004

Pope John Paul II, *Memory and Identity: Personal Reflections*, London: Weidenfeld & Nicholson, 2005

Pope John Paul II, *Redemptoris Mater*, Sydney: St Paul Publications, 1987

Hahn, Scott, *Hail Holy Queen: The Mother of God in the Word of God*, New York: Doubleday, 2001

Weigel, George, *Witness to Hope: The Biography of Pope John Paul II*, New York: Harper Collins, 1999